COLLINS POCKET REFERENCE

KW-051-624

STARTING YOUR OWN BUSINESS

Elaine Henderson and
Ronald McCorrisken

HarperCollins*Publishers*

HarperCollins Publishers
PO Box, Glasgow G4 0NB

First published 1997

Reprint 10 9 8 7 6 5 4 3 2 1 0

© Ronald McCorrisken and Elaine Henderson 1997

ISBN 0 00 471014 2

Every effort has been made to provide an up-to-date text but the publishers cannot accept any liability for errors, omissions or changes in detail or for any consequences arising from the use of information contained herein. The publishers welcome corrections and suggestions from readers. Write to:

Reference Department
HarperCollins Publishers
PO Box, Glasgow G4 0NB

Printed and bound in Great Britain by
Caledonian International Book Manufacturing Ltd, Glasgow G64

CONTENTS

INTRODUCTION

PART ONE   IS SELF-EMPLOYMENT RIGHT FOR YOU?   1

Chapter 1: The Thinking Stage   3

Is running my own business right for me?   4

Why start your own business?   6

What motivates you?   7

What are your aims and objectives?   8

How will you measure your success?   8

What business skills and experience do you have?   9

Your financial and administrative skills   10

It's all about – timing!   13

Who will be affected by your decision – and how?   14

Chapter 2: The Writing Stage   20

The Personal Summary   20

The Outline Business Plan   23

Review   32

PART TWO   STRUCTURING THE BUSINESS   37

Chapter 1: What kind of organization?   39

Chapter 2: What sources of money are available?   49

Chapter 3: Writing the Business Plan   76

CONTENTS

PART THREE   GETTING STARTED   133

     Chapter 1: Marketing and selling   135

     Chapter 2: Successful selling for beginners   150

     Chapter 3: Organizing your business   168

         1. The office   168

         2. Money matters   196

         3. Employing people   203

PART FOUR   STAYING IN BUSINESS!   215

APPENDIX   243

     Choosing your advisers   245

         List of useful organizations   251

         Specimen Contract of Employment   256

         Specimen Business Plan   272

INTRODUCTION

Most people dream at some point in their lives of running their own business, particularly when they're crawling through the Monday morning rush-hour traffic, had an argument with 'the boss' or have just been passed over for promotion. The appeal of choosing your own working hours, being responsible for your own decisions and organizing your day-to-day activities without consulting anyone else can be a powerful lure. But the plain fact is, that for most people becoming self-employed remains, and rightly remains, just that – a dream. For some, however, the dream slowly begins to take shape, becomes more realistic, less fantastic, and finally becomes a fact. Sometimes an external catalyst, such as redundancy or early retirement, catapults the dream into becoming reality; sometimes it's a slow process, evolving over years. But however it happens, starting your own business is a major, life-altering decision and should never been seen as an easy option to being employed.

The fact that you have invested money in this little book at least reveals that you are interested in finding out more about the facts and figures of starting a business for yourself. We will guide you through the various processes from analysing yourself and thinking about the impact self-employment will have on your life right through to tips on how to keep going once you've started. Although the book has a logical structure it can also be used as a reference guide to various aspects of the necessary preparation and fulfilment of your plan.

Self-employment is becoming increasingly popular as an alternative to full-time paid employment and, as the available number of good jobs diminishes as employers 'downsize', more and more people are deciding on the independent option. The growth in small businesses during the 1980s, with over 400,000 start-ups each year, led to a 70% increase in self-employment. There are now approximately 2.5 million businesses in the UK with some three million people describing themselves as self-employed. Most of these 2.5 million businesses consist of one or two people only. Alongside these encouraging statistics we must, of course, take into account those companies which fail.

The most vulnerable time for new companies is one to three years after start-up, but those which successfully negotiate the rocks and shallows of these early years have a high chance of survival. Business failure is often, but certainly not always, linked to financial difficulties – there are many other reasons for ceasing to trade and many businesses go on to survive financial problems and do not close.

In this book we suggest that careful and thorough financial planning and good management can help you to maintain constant control over the company's day-to-day situation so that you can take effective action BEFORE problems arise. And if you do run into difficulty there are several government and other agencies (see the list at the back of the book) which provide free, confidential help and advice for small businesses. Small businesses are now big business and the government is committed to encouraging even more people to leave conventional paid employment and to start up on their own. The fastest growing areas in the period 1979-1992 were finance, property, professional and business services followed by wholesaling. Depending on the individual circumstances, direct financial assistance, grants, training and counselling are all available through the various government agencies and thousands of people are helped every year.

Small businesses are certainly a force to be reckoned with today and are a powerful lobby; they show every sign of increasing their role within the social and economic life of the nation. So if, after careful thought and planning, you decide that self-employment is the right choice for you then Go for it – and Good Luck!

Ronald McCorrisken
Elaine Henderson

Acknowledgements

The authors would like to thank the following for giving us the benefit of their experience and expertise: Willy Anderson, Linda Barrett, David Burns, Chris Casely, Robert Dallas, Eddie Dec, Chris Devlin, Dougie Ferguson, John Flynn, Brian Glancey, Mark Hill, John Jackson, Stuart McAllister, Leisa McCracken, Helen Munro, Nick Patrick, Roddy Ramsay, Maureen Vaughn.

PART ONE

IS SELF-EMPLOYMENT
RIGHT FOR YOU?

1. THE THINKING STAGE

In this first section you should take the time to examine carefully your own motivations and feelings about why you are considering starting your own business. This major life decision will affect you, your family, your friends and the way you live. Go through the following suggestions carefully and in detail. You will discover more about yourself and come to realistic conclusions about your skills and your ability to put your plans into action. (A successful business depends very much on the owner's organizational abilities, personality and attitudes.) In addition, you will need the support of those around you, just as much as you need to have a good idea or to identify a niche in the market. Don't skim over this section – it may help you to spot potential weaknesses and pitfalls so that you can take effective action before you start putting your plans into force.

Although this section is designed to trigger off the thought process, you will find it extremely useful when you come to the next section, The Writing Stage, if you have jotted down notes of your answers and ideas as you have asked yourself the various questions raised.

Don't try to write long passages or even sentences yet, simply use key words or phrases which will remind you of ideas, and which could even be used as sub-headings, then expanded in detail at some point in the future.

e.g. Question: 'Why start my own business?'
       Answers: Need money/income
                  Success
                  Independence
                  Family life
                  Lifestyle   etc. etc. as appropriate to you.

Use the checklists provided as guides, but remember that this is for YOUR business future, so add or modify as you see fit.

1. Is running my own business right for me?

How well do you really know yourself? You should ask yourself 'Am I the right kind of person to be self-employed?' and analyse as objectively as you can those aspects of your experience, character and personality which will make or break you in business.

If you think that being in business for yourself is an easy alternative to being employed, you could be in for a nasty shock. In addition to all those skills which you call upon to carry out your normal employment, you will have to learn new skills and draw upon inner reserves just to survive on your own.

Now is the time to do some serious thinking about yourself: here are some questions to start you off.

	Yes	No

Are you in good health?

Is your age compatible with your
planned business?

Can you handle stress?

Do you enjoy responsibility?

Can you cope with loneliness?

Can you motivate yourself?

Can you live with financial
uncertainty?

Would you be willing to accept a
reduced income?

Can you maintain your self-belief in
the face of serious setbacks?

Can you cope with rejection?

Can you take decisions?

Do you get on well with people?

Are you a good communicator?

Can you work on your own, without
supervision?

Can you manage and motivate people?

Are you patient?

Are you a good salesman/woman?

Are you confident enough to take this risk?

Are you ambitious?

Are you a disciplined person?

Do you pay attention to detail?

Do you want to maximise your income?

If you have answered 'no' to most of these questions, perhaps you should rethink your ambitions to become self-employed. It is a fact that most people are unsuited to running their own business, for various reasons, and would be happier in employment. If you have answered 'yes' to most of these questions, then it is time to look a little more closely at your motivations and ask yourself why you want to become self-employed.

2. Why start your own business?

For some people the idea of having their own business is a dream which gives them the strength to sustain themselves during their daily working life, and provides them with hope of an escape route to an independent future lifestyle. There, they imagine, they can be free of the restraints which currently hold them back from enjoying life to the full, or even just free to do their job efficiently, without interference from bosses. The dream of being in business is sufficient for some, but for others there is a genuine desire to break away from their current situation.

Starting a business could be a short-term solution, to enable anyone affected by redundancy or early retirement to supplement their income, before re-entering employment. This kind of business often takes a form similar to that of employment, providing one's labour or skills for a fee, but with little prospect of a continuing or long-term relationship with that source of income (specialist consultancy, freelance book-keeping, photography, window cleaning, motor repairs, etc.). Of course, it may well be that the varied nature of this type of work, or the avoidance of long-term commitment (hence independence) is what makes it attractive in the first place.

Some long-established businesses began as short-term income earners, and grew until their own momentum made it almost impossible to stop. You can usually find examples of these in your local area, such as building firms which are now substantial operations and significant employers.

There are even some businesses which were set up because, basically, the proprietor was UNEMPLOYABLE in the eyes of others. He/she was left with the option of a drawn-out search for suitable employment or setting up a business, and it is fortunate for their employees that the independent route was chosen.

There are businesses which exist because the prime mover, i.e. the founder, was motivated by money or ego. In other words, to earn his or her fortune, be the boss and be respected for their achievements and success.

3. What motivates you?

In order to derive the most benefit and enjoyment from your own business, it is crucial to look objectively at the situation in which you find yourself, and ask yourself what you want from your life in general. If you know what your personal goals are, then it is easier to set out those milestones by which you can

measure your commercial and business success. Remember –
list what YOU want to get out of this adventure, not just the
things which you think that others might use as a measure of
your business success.

4. What are your aims and objectives?
Here are some suggestions to start you off:

	Yes	No
Freedom to get the job done		
Do the job better		
Concentrate on core functions/tasks		
Freedom from bureaucracy		
Freedom from workmates		
Freedom from bosses		
Earn more money		
Build a team		
Work flexible hours		
Earn £ XXX,XXX per annum		
Doing the job I enjoy MY way		
Get a job!		

5. How will you measure your success?

	Yes	No
New car		
Bigger house		

Earning £XXX,XXX per annum
Opening a factory
Opening a factory named after you
Establishing a family firm for future
   generations
Building an empire
Becoming famous
Becoming rich
Becoming powerful and
   influential
Getting by
Playing golf more often
Taking more holidays
Taking fewer holidays
Supporting the family more comfortably
Retire early and live in the sun
Spend more time in the garden

Is it important to you that others see you as successful, or are you happy to keep your success under wraps? Does material success take precedence over job satisfaction, or vice versa?

6. What business skills and experience do you have?

Now that you have reached this stage you will understand a great deal more about yourself, your motivations, aims and objectives. Now turn your attention to your business skills and experience.

Ask yourself the following questions:

What are the relevant educational qualifications/expertise you can offer?

How many years' experience have you had in your chosen field?

What relevant work have you done in this field?

What relevant training courses have you completed?

What is your current work situation?

At work, what are your responsibilities, and how are these relevant to your new business?

Are you a good communicator?

What talents/interests/hobbies have you that can help you in this business?

Can you offer reliable opinions in your chosen field which will be respected by others?

Many businesses can be founded on general experience or common sense, rather than specific training or expertise, e.g. cleaning services, bed and breakfast accommodation, chauffeur drive. However, invest in training and development and you could provide an even better service!

7. Your financial and administrative abilities

Most businesses which fail do so because of a lack of planning and/or financial control, or poor administration. It is not sufficient to be an excellent carpenter if your business is to survive and flourish. If you neglect the administration of your business it will almost certainly come back to haunt you at the most inconvenient time.

Look at the comparisons below and answer the questions HONESTLY - this is for your own benefit, and will show you how much (or how little) knowledge or experience you have of financial and administrative matters. Take stock of this now, because without SOMEONE taking care of the administration, the effect could be disastrous!

Which sounds more like you?

Do you have:

a.   A simple method of household bill management?
     or
b.   Debts which are getting out of control?(e.g. credit cards, bills, car loans?)

a.   A well-organized personal filing system
     or
b.   No idea where to find your driving licence, birth certificate, NI number or passport?

a.   A savings account where you make regular deposits
     or
b.   A small stash of cash somewhere at home, but not sure how much or where?

If you lean more towards (a) answers than (b), you could probably cope quite well on your own initially. If you lean more towards (b) than (a) then you need a lot of help! With the assistance of your accountant or business adviser you can set up a fairly simple system to keep control of the paperwork. For the less adept at book-keeping, this can even take the shape of collecting all your receipts and other paperwork in a shoebox, and letting your accountant or book-keeper sort it out for you. It has to be said that even in these days of advanced technology, the shoe-box system is alive and well! On a more serious note, you must work at keeping records as up-to-date as possible.

Do not despair. As you will learn:

CASH IS KING!

With enough money in your 'war chest' or fund to start your business, it is possible to buy in most of the expertise required to set up and run a successful operation. You must take into account the cost of such expertise when you are working out your business plan and finances. Make contact with a suitable accountant, preferably by personal referral from someone who uses that firm, and establish a likely charge for providing the range of services which your business will require on an ongoing basis. (Get a quote for any likely extra work, such as unravelling your box of receipts each week.) Do not forget that you will need to have your end-of-year accounts prepared for taxation purposes and inspection by the Inland Revenue and

Customs and Excise (for VAT), which will probably include an audit, if you operate a limited company. You may not like the charges involved, or the amount of time you might have to spend on this yourself, but they are necessary evils.

The creator of a business, the person with the driving force that turns the idea into reality, and the overwhelming enthusiasm of that individual, can often compensate for most of the myriad mistakes that will inevitably be made on the road to success. But if you can carefully analyse your own skills in these areas and compare them to the potential needs of the business at this stage, you will soon see where the 'skills gap' lies and can take action to plug it successfully. It is not necessary to become a 'Jack (or Jill) of all trades', just be aware that financial control and tight administration are vitally important for a successful business and you will have to pay for these skills if you are not able, prepared, or qualified to include them in your day-to-day work.

For example, most sales-oriented people (R. McCorrisken included!) tend to be disinclined towards paperwork or book-keeping, and experience shows that the best salesmen or saleswomen do not necessarily make the best sales managers, but often make excellent trainers in that specialist area.

8. It's all about – Timing!

Be realistic! Is the world really ready at the moment for an electronic widget detector? Does your idea already exist elsewhere? Has someone already tried and failed in a similar project? If so, find out why it failed, and profit from someone else's mistakes and experience.

Bear in mind that most businesses struggle or fail because of a lack of funding at the very start. Do not be tempted to launch too soon in the hope that you'll find the rest of the money somehow in the future, especially if the downside risk of getting it wrong means the collapse of the business and the loss of your house!

Is the time right for you personally? If you are pressurized, for whatever reason, into starting your business before you are ready, then the chances of failure dramatically increase. If you do not feel in control and confident at the start, you will be easily discouraged or defeated by the negative aspects of business which you will quickly encounter. Get into the driving seat, and start as you mean to go on.

9. Who will be affected by your decision – and how?
Becoming self-employed is a major life decision and your work will impinge upon every facet of your life. Before you go any further, you should take the time to consider the serious implications of becoming self-employed on you and everyone close to you.

You – You probably won't notice the changes, but your friends and family definitely will. Here's how A views the changes in her boyfriend:

'He started to become more irritable, and his mood could change more dramatically than before he became involved in the business. He was unable to switch off after work the way that he used to, and his working day became much longer, and the working week stretched into the weekends. Because he was responsible for the buildings that the company owned, or were working on, he'd wake up in a panic if there were high winds and heavy rain, and even drive around the area in his car to check on them in the middle of the night. He had to get his dentist to make a protective plate for him to wear at night because he was grinding his teeth away to nothing while he was sleeping!'

Partners – If you have a spouse or other partner in your life, he or she will be the first person to be affected by your actions. The effects will be not only financial if income stops or slows down in the early stages. Your partner will think that he or she is living with a different person! The all-encompassing nature of your business will probably occupy your every waking moment in the early stages, and, as we have seen above, probably many of your sleeping moments too!

B says of her husband:

'I got used to the idea that he wouldn't be working regular hours, and would often be away during the week or sometimes over the weekend. Although it's good to see the business doing well, it means that you don't have as much time together as you would like, and you have to have your own social circle so that you don't lose touch with your friends. You even find yourself wishing that he could just get an ordinary job and settle down, so that we could do ordinary things together like dig the garden or paint the house!'

Since you are likely to have to pledge your home as security, any co-owner, probably your spouse or live-in partner, will have to agree and sign the documentation. It is essential that your spouse is aware of the possible implications of doing so, i.e. that if the business fails and there are insufficient funds to repay the bank, there is a possibility that the house might have to be sold to meet your debt to the bank. In addition, even if it is not specifically pledged, other creditors (people owed money by the business) will have a call on the house and all other assets of all business partners in order to try and recoup their money from you, if you have unlimited liability, i.e. as a sole trader or partner. This can put intense strain on a relationship.

Your spouse or live-in partner will not enjoy watching you burn the candle at both ends, and suffer from fatigue, no matter how rosy a future you think it will bring! He or she will be supportive up to the point where it is obvious that your health is suffering through overwork.

Discussing your plans fully and realistically with your partner and keeping him/her informed on the progress of the business can help to prevent resentment and pressure building up. Many homes have been broken because of the problems resulting from the stresses of self-employment, but you can help to avoid this by making sure your partner knows what is happening – and an understanding and supportive partner/family can be of invaluable help. In addition, your home life should be relatively stable and without major concerns such as unmanageable debts, difficult children, long-term sickness before you consider starting your business.

Remember that if you are working from home, you owe it to your partner and family to try to separate home life from business life. It will not be appreciated in the slightest if you have people coming and going at all hours of the day and night to talk about business, especially if your spouse finds that he/she is confronted by business guests in the sittingroom every time he/she goes in! Keep business papers and clutter to a minimum, and try to ensure that there is a designated place to work and talk business, if at all possible, to avoid swamping your home and family with things which are essential to you but irrelevant to them.

Children – How will you feel if little Johnny is aching for the latest day-glo, light-emitting virtual reality helmet and gloves, and you honestly cannot afford this type of indulgence for the first time in years? The office telephone bill will have to take priority at times like this. And of course, it's also a question of time: do you attend the school sports day, Saturday hockey or football, when the time could be spent profitably tidying up paperwork, submitting VAT returns or dealing with customers instead.

Parents – Remember that as your parents get older they may not enjoy the same rude health of their younger days, and will possibly put a greater demand on your time than before. They may resent the fact that you don't visit or help them as much as you used to, and may not appreciate the pressure that you are under. They will, however, be able to point out to you how much you are neglecting your partner/family/self. Try to take heed without taking offence. You can help to avoid bad feeling and resentment building up by discussing your plans and their implications fully with your parents before you start, and by keeping them informed of your progress. Parents worry about their children long after they are grown up and they want you to be happy – so keep them involved and they will probably give you much-needed support and encouragement.

Friends – What an excellent source of support and comfort for the self-employed! Why then do they generally get neglected so much? Try to keep in regular contact with your social circle, but don't rely on them trying to include you in everything. They will soon get fed up if you fail to show at various events you've been invited to, and the invitations will then become less frequent. If you have a partner or spouse, your friends will become even more important for them. Don't forget that sports and social clubs are also excellent ways of making business contacts or entertaining business clients, but avoid the temptation of ramming business down the throat of all your friends at every turn.

Pets – Will you be too busy or too tired to walk the dog, feed the budgie or brush the cat? How will you feel when the dog barks warningly to protect your family when you walk wearily up the driveway?

2. THE WRITING STAGE

If you have followed the thinking process suggested in Chapter One, you should now have a much clearer picture of why you want to work for yourself, your skills and abilities and your possible areas of weakness. You will have thought carefully about the impact of your decision on your own life and on the lives of those around you.

The Writing Stage takes this process one stage further and consist of two main elements: your Personal Summary and the Outline Business Plan.

1.The Personal Summary
Why do I need a Personal Summary?
You may have noticed the increasing trend for companies and organizations in all sectors, but especially those in the public eye, to publish a 'mission statement' or 'customer charter'. These statements are found on their brochures, prospectuses and even on the annual accounts. The 'mission statement' is intended to express the organization's idea of its function and purpose, and the goals it hopes to achieve (commercial or otherwise).

Your Personal Summary will, in the same way, become your own personal 'mission statement', providing you with a constant reference point; it will remind you why you wanted to go into business in the first place and what you hoped to achieve.

As the business begins to take shape you can refer back to the Statement and see whether you are drifting away from your original focus, and why, and whether your initial thoughts were hopelessly optimistic or over-cautious.

Your Personal Summary can also act as a 'reality check', to bring you down to earth a little and to act as a steadying force if, in the initial heady days of enthusiasm, you are in danger of being carried away or, alternatively, if an unforeseen event brings you close to despair!

What do I put in my Summary?

The Personal Summary should be no longer than a single page – it is intended to capture the essence of your aims, not to examine them in detail. You may like to use the tried and tested 'who, what, why, when, where and how' formula or you could write two or three short paragraphs setting out your general aims and ambitions, how you intend to achieve them and the estimated time scale involved. Your Personal Summary will also help you when you come to prepare your Business Plan. Once you have written your Personal Summary you should pin a copy somewhere visible, e.g. on the wall in the area where you work, to act as a constant reminder for you.

SAMPLE PERSONAL SUMMARY/MISSION STATEMENT

My aim is to establish a profitable, home-based consultancy business, offering clients an independent and objective review of their hairdressing salons and the quality of their service.

The business I create will allow me to work flexible hours and this will mean that I can enjoy both work and family life.

The initial savings in child-minding fees will mean that I can afford to take a drop in gross salary in Year One from £18000 to £13000 without affecting my standard of living.

In Year Two I want to earn £20000 which will mean a slightly improved standard of living, and I hope to employ a part-time assistant to help cope with increased turnover.

During that year I will probably move into business premises such as the local business centre, to allow me to control the paperwork and ensure that home life is not disrupted too much by the additional team member.

In Year Three I hope to have sufficient business to recruit a further part-time assistant, and promote the first team member to full-time, if to our mutual benefit. I will make him/her responsible for organizing the workload for us all, as well as continuing to promote the business via sales letters and telephone follow-up calls.

2. The Outline Business Plan
What is a Business Plan?
A Business Plan is a document that describes the proposed commercial and financial operations of an enterprise, accompanied by a detailed breakdown of supporting information, usually presented as Appendices.

Why do I need a Business Plan?
Many people believe that Business Plans are only required when someone wishes to borrow money for a project and that they are prepared as purely financial documents. Although this is partly true all potential business owners should prepare a business plan as, first and foremost, a management tool. It serves to focus, in an organized way, on the objectives, risks and potential success of the business. The Business Plan is the most crucial document that you will prepare for your business, whether or not you are using it to attract capital investment. In this section we look at the broader issues involved in preparing a Business Plan and the work you do on your Outline Business Plan will serve as the basis for the more detailed information you will need if you intend to present a formal Business Plan to a potential lender. (Help on writing a formal Business Plan will be found in Part Two, Chapter Three).

• The length, depth, breadth and detail of your business plan will depend on many factors, not least of which is the amount of money you are trying to raise from investors, lenders and grant-donating bodies.

- It is also an important document for you as it will contain your justification for investing not only your own money, but your LIFE in the project.

- It should be written in terms that are easily understood by a layperson, with little or no experience of your chosen field. Jargon should be avoided wherever possible, or at least clearly explained if unavoidable.

Although you will probably be fired with enthusiasm at this early stage and may even envisage dashing off your Outline Business Plan in a few hours, this will just not be possible. Many hours of thinking, planning, writing and rewriting will be necessary if you are to present your business proposals in the best possible light. This Outline stage will be an invaluable help when you come to write the 'real thing'.

> Professional business advisers agree that a lack of planning is a significant factor in the failure of many enterprises. 'FAIL TO PLAN - PLAN TO FAIL'.

Of course, if you are fortunate enough not to need to borrow money for your project, your Outline Business Plan will suffice for management purposes, but you should still take the time and trouble to prepare it thoroughly: it will help to crystallize your ideas and act as a guiding strategy through the early stages after start-up.

Where do I start?

Your Outline Business Plan should show that:

1. You have a clearly defined idea of how you see your business at the start and what you expect it to become. (Introduction)

2. You understand all about your product or service and how to market it. (Business Strategy)

3. You, and any others involved in the enterprise, are experienced and capable of managing it. (Management)

4. You have researched the current and potential markets for your product/service. (Marketing)

5. You have taken into account the risk factors most likely to affect the business. (Principal Risks)

6. You have prepared Profit and Loss and Cash Flow forecasts and you have investigated the most appropriate methods of funding the business. (Finance)

7. You have prepared a summary of the viability of the business. (Conclusion)

Now we will look at these points in greater detail.

Introduction

This should be no more than a one- or two-page summary at the most, and should contain information about you, your background and experience (the notes you made during the Thinking Stage will help you here). Next, state clearly what kind of business you want to run and why you think you will be able to make a success of it. Include here details of your existing expertise which relates to the proposed business and show how you intend to gain any necessary skills which you presently lack. You should also outline the management structure and give information on premises and relevant machinery, equipment and services available. Finally, you can indicate any need for additional capital investment for equipment/premises/running costs and how you intend to find the money for these.

Business Strategy

Here you can show how thoroughly you understand your product or service, and how you intend to penetrate the market and make a profit. Explain the advantages that your product/service has over its competitors and how you propose to target and sell your product/service to the appropriate purchaser.

Sales strategy and pricing policy also come in here and should be explained, comparing them with that of your competitors. Finally you should demonstrate how these policies will enable you to make a profit and increase your market share.

Management

Many businesses fail because of poor management, and potential lenders will be particularly keen to know how your business is structured. Even if you are a 'one man' or 'one woman' business, you still need to show how the day to day management of the enterprise will be carried out; correspondence, book-keeping, invoicing, banking, dealing with suppliers and so on. In such a case the lender will want to know about accounting procedures and that you have made adequate arrangements for keeping the business accounts in good order, most probably by using the services of a book-keeper or accountant. If the business is a larger concern and there will be two or more partners or employees, the role of each, together with an outline of their skills and experience, should be given.

Marketing

Here you need to demonstrate that you have a well-thought-out marketing strategy which will show that:

- there is a definite demand for your product/service;

- you understand the nature of your product/service thoroughly (see **Business Strategy** above);

- you believe in its potential.

Market sizes and trends can also be analysed and you can give a forecast as to the possible future growth of the market. You should also indicate that you have planned a marketing and advertising campaign (brochures, leaflets, newspaper advertising, posters, flyers, direct mail, 'cold calling' etc.) that is appropriate to your enterprise and likely to give the best results.

For more detailed information on marketing, turn to Part Two, Chapter Three, *Writing the Business Plan*, and to Part Three, Chapter One, *Marketing and Selling*.

Principal Risks

Perhaps the simplest way of dealing with this section is to ask yourself 'What Would Happen If ......?'

- Sales were lower or higher than predicted

- Invoices were not settled within 60 days (or expected credit terms)

- I lost a major customer

- My partner became ill

- Interest rates suddenly rose dramatically

- My main supplier went bankrupt

- A new competitor undercut my prices

By asking and answering such questions you will gain an insight into the possible risks your business could face - and any potential lender will certainly want to question you on such eventualities. Each business will have its own relevant inherent risks and you should note these and show how you would deal with them. Include as much detail as necessary and BE HONEST with yourself.

Finance

The key element here is the Cash Flow Forecast, that is, your financial predictions for the first two-three years of your project's life. By taking a number of years as a starting point you can demonstrate the estimated financial stability of your enterprise. Supply careful assessments of the total anticipated income and expenditure for each year. Of course these figures (your Cash Flow Forecast) will only be estimates, but you should be prepared to justify them. Again, you must be honest with predictions: wildly optimistic forecasts will do nothing to convince potential investors of your business acumen. In Part Two, Chapter Three, *Writing the Business Plan*, we cover the financial aspects of starting a business in much greater depth, and this includes a guide to creating a Cash Flow Forecast and a sample Forecast.

> Remember, a Cash Flow Forecast is not a Profit Forecast. It simply indicates the estimated movements of money in terms of income and expenditure of a business over a period of time; NOT the profit.

You will possibly need to raise some capital to start off your business and will have investigated the most appropriate sources of finance already, probably one (or more) of the following:

(a) Banks – Normally 'High Street' i.e. your local branch of a major bank, but sometimes merchant banks;

(b) Institutional Investors – pension funds and insurance companies, for example. Usually interested in larger investments, in the £ millions;

(c) Private Lenders – Family, friends or third parties known or introduced to the entrepreneur as interested in assisting small businesses to get started, usually for a higher than normal rate of return;

(d) Private Investors – Same sources as (c) above, but possibly over a longer term, therefore these investments can often be 'sweetened' by the use of specifically introduced tax incentives, such as the Enterprise Investment Scheme. Sometimes known as Business Angels;

(e) Venture Capitalists – There is a recognized body of private or independent Venture Capital Organizations in the UK, as well as bodies such as Investors in Industry (3i) which used to be owned by the major banks, but was floated on the stock market recently;

(f) Grant Sources – the Department of Trade and Industry (DTI) is the main UK reference point for European Union (EU) grants, but there is also a plethora of other sources of help, known variously as Local Enterprise Trusts, Enterprise Companies, Business Shops etc. (The List of Useful Organizations in the Appendix gives more information on these.)

To attract the serious interest of any of the above in your enterprise, you will need to understand their aims and objectives, a little of how each body operates, and at what financial level. This avoids wasting your time, or theirs, with an inappropriate proposal. More details on each can be found in

Part Two, Chapter Two, *The Money – What Sources are Available?*

Conclusion

This can describe what you hope to have achieved in your business in two to three years. You can outline your short- and long-term ambitions and aims and can show your drive and determination. Keep the Conclusion fairly short and, again, be REALISTIC. This is the part that people will read to get a grasp of your idea; try to make it as effective as possible.

Following through these seven stages will give you your Outline Business Plan. If you are fortunate enough not to need to borrow any money, this Outline Business Plan should suffice as a statement of intent for your business, and a valuable reference point once you have started. Ask interested friends and third parties to look it over and suggest areas which might need further thought or more detail.

If you need to approach a potential lender then you will need a more detailed Business Plan, particularly with respect to the financial information and profit forecasts. However, the work you have done on the Outline Business Plan can be used to provide the basic information and the Appendices which will accompany your formal Business Plan. Help in compiling and presenting a Business Plan will be found in Part Two, Chapter Three.

3. Review

Before moving on to the next stage it is worthwhile taking a step back and comparing your Personal Summary with the results of your soul-searching for your Outline Business Plan.

- Are the two documents actually compatible?

- Does your Summary still contain valid and realistic objectives?

- Do you still think that you want to go ahead with your idea?

- Be honest, could you really still be bothered with all the aggravation, and make a go of it?

- If your answer is 'Yes!' to all these, then press on!

If you find that you are out of step with your original concept, try to identify why this is the case, and go back over your original notes to help you find the reasons why. Many people in the past have started a business for which they weren't really prepared, and some suffered dire consequences. The fact that you've taken the trouble to come this far probably means that you've got what it takes to make it on your own, it's just a question of when. If you've the maturity to stop yourself now and wait until the moment is right, you'll be glad you didn't start too soon.

But for those whose enthusiasm is unabated after all this work, the next stage is even more work, because there is still a great deal of planning and preparation to do before that magical day when you open the doors of your own business for the very first time. In the next sections we look in detail at the two most important aspects of organizing the business: Structure and Finance.

CASE HISTORY
John, Chiropodist

I started out on my own straight after qualifying so I've never worked for anyone else. At the time I had quite a lot of work referred to me by the NHS and that helped me to survive while I was building up my private client base. That doesn't happen now. I managed to build up the practice to the extent that my appointment books were full and I was going straight from one client to the next. The result was that I was exhausted at the end of each day but I still wasn't making the kind of money consistent with such hard work.

I decided to go on a short Business Management Course run by my professional association, and discovered that several other people were in the same position. The advice given to us was that we were all charging too little. I could see the sense in this but I felt that my clients would not see it the same way and would leave me in droves! The day after I came back from the course I raised my fees, although I was very nervous about it. But, to my surprise, I only lost about two percent of my clients overall. That relatively small rise enabled me to cut my workload so I felt much better and was earning more. I now raise my fees regularly to keep abreast of market value.

The only really difficult period came when my accountant, whom I trusted implicitly, over-claimed travel expenses for home visits on my tax return. I probably should have seen this, but I didn't, and the Inland Revenue asked me to justify these. Of course I realized then what had happened but my accountant disappeared overnight and I had to handle the matter myself. In the end the bank threatened to bankrupt me for £3000 unpaid tax and I had to borrow money from my parents. If they hadn't been able to lend me the cash I'd have lost everything.

My advice to anyone starting up on their own would be to get a really good and trustworthy accountant and be prepared to pay for their work. You also have to go into your tax returns thoroughly yourself so you know exactly what's happening. I don't regret working for myself and I'd do it again – it lets me control my own working life and make my own decisions. I don't think I'd be happy working for anyone else.

PART TWO

STRUCTURING
THE
BUSINESS

1. WHAT KIND OF ORGANIZATION?

In this chapter we will look at the probable advantages and disadvantages of limited and unlimited liability structures, paying particular attention to minimizing the financial risks to you and your family, as well as to lenders and investors.

Sole Trader (Self employed status).
Designation: e.g. Smith & Co.
Many small businesses begin and continue to operate in this way. It is the simplest, fastest and cheapest way to get started, but it is also potentially risky. As the sole proprietor of the business, you have the dubious honour of carrying the responsibility for the payment of all business debts (e.g. suppliers, VAT, tax, bank) from your personal resources in the event that your business is unable to meet its obligations for whatever reason. Despite this potentially onerous burden, if you plan to operate in a low-risk environment or where the major exposure to risk can be insured (e.g. public/employers liability, sales/credit risks) it may well be the option for you. There may also be future tax advantages to transfer your business into a limited company, particularly if your main business asset has accrued a substantial potential capital gain, e.g. the value of your business property has increased since the date of original purchase.

If you intend to operate in a field where little capital is required, but where there is a potential risk of substantial personal liability if things go wrong, you will need to consider carefully the protection of your personal assets, particularly your home, well in advance. If your major assets are not required or are already fully committed to support borrowings from sources such as the bank, it might be feasible to legitimately transfer any interest which you might have to your spouse or children, for example.

Consult your solicitor or accountant before doing so, to avoid possible come-backs later. Remember, though, that this is often the main or only source of security for any bank lending (No Security No Loan, despite what the banks might say at your first meeting).

Provided you carefully consider all the possible repercussions of a transfer of assets, and it is done properly (allowing the minimum requisite time to elapse, for example), this has the advantage of removing your home from the list of potential areas of attack by creditors in the event of the business failing. At least it ensures that you would not immediately lose your home as well as your business.

Partnership (Self employed partner status) Designation: Smith & Jones
What is a Partner?

It is someone who has a direct involvement in the running of your business, who owns some percentage of the business, and who shares in the profits and losses generated therein. This is fine when matters are going well, but in fact you and your partner(s) are likely to be 'jointly and severally' (ie equally) responsible for the debts of the business in the event of it failing. What this means for you is that if your erstwhile partner proves to have been hopelessly incompetent (or even dishonest) but has disposed of, transferred or squandered all his personal fortune before plunging the business into a downward spiral, then the creditors (people or businesses owed money by your company) are quite entitled to pursue you for payment. Your liability is, in theory, unlimited, and you could lose your house, stocks and shares, villa in Spain and, possibly, some gold fillings (only joking!) to pay for your partner's misdemeanours. Be careful!

Partnerships are particularly common in the professions, e.g. lawyers and accountants. The function of each partner can be adjusted by the Partnership Agreement, which states clearly the responsibilities of each partner, and their contributions to/awards from the business. It is essential to have a properly drawn-up agreement, preferably drafted by a lawyer with wide experience in these matters.

Partnerships are fine until things go wrong: ask anyone who's been in one.

Private Limited Company (Director/employee status) Designation: Smith, Jones Limited (or Ltd)

In the UK you can set up a private limited company with a share capital of as little as you like, providing that there are two ordinary shares issued to different subscribers. The normal value of these shares is £1 each, so you could join the ranks of many thousands of shareholders and owner/managers for the princely sum of £1. Many small companies are started in this way, but gradually increase the amount of shares subscribed.

A director may lend money to his company and charge interest on the loan. The sum remains repayable, and it will be shown in the company's accounts as Director's Loan Account. However, you will find that banks would prefer you to convert these loans to capital, i.e. investment in equity, which is not repayable, in order to 'strengthen the balance sheet', and to show long-term commitment.

> Where you wish to keep the executive management to a husband and wife (or similar partnership arrangement), try to avoid the temptation for both parties to be directors. It would probably be better for the party who is less involved on a day-to-day basis to be the Company Secretary. Although still an officer of the company, the liabilities are less, and the Company Secretary is not normally required to give bank guarantees.

It is not necessary for a shareholder to be a director, or for a director to be a shareholder. Where there are two spouses, or a similar modern relationship, shares tend to be held by each party, to fulfil the requirement for two initial subscribers. Once the company is formed, it is possible for all shares to be held by only one party. However, in doing so, that party then runs the risk of exposing himself or herself to unlimited liability in the event of the company failing. This is a point which is extremely important and should be discussed fully with an adviser before effecting such a shareholding.

In practice, the owner/manager of a limited liability company will find that, if borrowing from a bank, it is still necessary to provide that lender with adequate security, usually in the form of a charge over the main family home of ALL the directors or AT LEAST of the main director. This effectively means that your liability extends beyond the initial value of your share subscription, and you could still find your home at risk even if you have chosen the limited company route.

One point about limited companies is that the UK system can work against you, because you will probably find one day that you have supplied your products or services to someone, a limited company, who is unable to pay and who might then go into liquidation. You will become very upset indeed when you discover that this person is still living a normal life, and possibly even setting up a similar operation to take over where the old one left off, while you and many other creditors do not receive a penny in compensation for the old business transactions, but must scrabble around trying to salvage your business. This is the commercial risk which you will face every day, and it is up to you thoroughly to check the credit-worthiness of each client before getting too heavily involved. There are several ways of doing this, including using a credit reference agency, getting details of a company's structure and finance from Companies House (see the address list at the end of the book), or simply asking for trade references, preferably from someone that you know. The most commonly used method is to ask for their bank details, and getting your bank to ask for an opinion from their bank. None of these provides any guarantee for you, but helps minimize risks.

If you have chosen to borrow for your business from the same source that has provided you with your personal mortgage, you might be surprised to find that the lender has not insisted on a second charge over your home as security for the further loan, only a personal guarantee by you, the director. Far from getting off scot-free from providing any security, you will probably find that your existing mortgage agreement contains an 'all sums due' clause. This means that if the bank has reason to call in the amount which you have guaranteed and you are unable to stump up the cash there and then, the bank has the right to repossess your home and sell it to realize the repayment of the mortgage, and also of that sum which you have guaranteed for your business loan. If possible, avoid this situation by using altogether separate personal and business lenders.

Every year, companies must file accounts at the Companies House where they were registered. Accounts tend to be audited by chartered accountants to confirm their validity, but there are now certain exceptions for smaller companies. The information filed here forms the basis for any credit checking by credit reference agencies. In addition, there is a requirement to file an annual return, showing the shareholding of the company, a list of directors and the company secretary. Any other directorships held by the directors currently or in the last 5 years should also be shown on the annual return form, allowing a better picture to be formed of the individuals concerned. Private addresses should also be shown, but there is now a move afoot to change this, instigated by wealthy or prominent directors of large companies fearing kidnap or terrorist assault.

Public Limited Companies (Director/employee status) Designation: Smith & Jones PLC

It is possible to set up a Public Limited Company with only £12,500 value of share issued. It is done very simply in much the same way as setting up a Private Limited Company; it costs the same, but has different accounting and reporting requirements.

We are not talking about the PLC companies listed on the stock exchange, only companies whose memorandum and articles of association (or constitution, if you like) allow the public issue of shares, as opposed to the private issue of shares.

There can be certain benefits in using a PLC status, such as:

• adding a degree of prestige to the company's title;

- showing trading partners that you have at least capitalized the company at a decent level;

- forcing a discipline upon your company of preparing annual accounts faster (a PLC is only allowed seven months maximum from year end to file accounts; a Private Limited Company has ten months).

However, there may also be the following disadvantages:

- becoming a source of amusement for people who know the extent of your PLC status, and who think you're trying to 'show off';

- confusing trading partners into thinking you can afford more than you really can;

- larger fines for late filing of accounts. (You pay the same penalties as international companies, but they can better afford them!)

Franchising

Franchising is a method of commercial operation which runs on the basis that one party (the franchisor) has developed a successful business which is then franchised (or licensed) to the second party (the franchisee) to start and run in a designated area for a designated period. Fast-food restaurants and printing and photocopying outlets are particularly well established in this field.

The main advantages of franchising are that the franchisor:

- has already solved most of the initial problems involved in setting up a business;

- can offer expert advice and assistance;

- has already made his or her business a proven success and may have a well-known name which will help in raising funds and attracting customers.

The main disadvantages are:

- taking a franchise can be expensive; there is an initial fee to the franchisor (often several thousand pounds), normal start-up costs and a regular percentage payable to the franchisor from income;

- you will have limited control over the business and how it develops;

- you are very dependent on the goodwill of the franchisor for continuing help.

Contact the British Franchise Association (address at your local library) for advice and consult your solicitor and local business enterprise office. Taking a franchise might well be the best option for you, but it needs just as much careful thought and planning as starting up on your own, and is definitely not an easy option.

> Don't forget – a franchisor is in business to make a profit from the franchisees!

Co-operatives

If you are reluctant to take the huge step of launching out on your own, then why not consider a co-operative structure? Co-operatives are owned equally by everyone who works there, from the chief executive to the cleaner, and decisions are taken democratically. Wholefood co-operatives, for example, have become established in many cities in recent years. A Community Business operates in much the same way, except that it is owned by a community – either of people living in the same area or of people holding a common interest.

Co-operatives can register as a co-operative society or can be a partnership or limited company.

2. WHAT SOURCES OF MONEY ARE AVAILABLE?

It's not uncommon for someone to start a business even before they've given much thought to the financing requirements of that fledgling enterprise. Within a few short months, weeks or even days, however, they often run into a financial brick wall. At that point, they might have to stand back and watch while their business collapses, out of control, possibly with disastrous consequences for their home and family life.

The main point which will come out of this section is that all potential sources of finance should be thoroughly investigated, if at all possible, before starting the business. In many cases, it will be in the interests of the potential entrepreneur to 'keep his/her powder dry' and conserve all possible funds until the appropriate package can be assembled in full. Certain sources of grant aid (free money, remember) can only assist if the business has not commenced. Once an application has been made to such a source, the project, or at least that part of it to which the grant is relevant, must not begin without the consent of the grant awarding body. If in doubt – ask!

Raising finance for a small business can be a long, difficult and sometimes soul-destroying task. You will think that the amount of effort required on your part is completely out of proportion to the amount of money sought. Believe it or not, it can be easier to raise £5 million than it is to raise £50,000 in many cases, providing that the project can justify it! You would be well advised to make enquiries to a number of advisory sources regarding the scale you envisage for your project, to ensure that you're going about it the best way, both in terms of the market potential and the attractiveness to lenders or investors. If you are unsure which potential investors to approach, then consult your local business development centre (see list at the end of this book), your bank manager, accountant or other professional adviser.

If at all possible, try to establish more than one source of finance to ensure a 'safety net' for yourself in case your primary source changes the rules of its involvement. This might even include a credit card with a useful (and available) credit limit for use in a TEMPORARY EMERGENCY only.

Before you go any further, however, there are three crucial questions you should ask yourself:

- How much will I need to borrow?

- What can I offer as security?

- When do I want my business to start?

How much will I need to borrow?

If you have prepared your Outline Business Plan carefully you will see at a glance broadly the level of finance needed so that your business can get off the ground and progress to the point where it can sustain itself. Some businesses are 'cash rich' and can become self-sufficient very quickly, but others will take longer to get into a cycle which is sustainable.

In order to decide how much you need to borrow, you need to establish how much money you, and others, have available to invest as Equity.

- Equity Finance is, basically, the amount of money the owner and other investors (usually as shareholders), have put into the company. Unlike a loan, Equity Finance does not have to be repaid, but investors usually expect some kind of return through dividend payments on the company's profits and an increase in the value of the shares. Generally, no interest is payable on ordinary Equity Finance, but there is a class of shares, known as preference shares, which bear interest like a loan.

- Debt Finance is the amount of money borrowed by a company from a lender or lenders who expect to be repaid. Money can be borrowed on a short-term basis (e.g. overdraft) or medium to longer-term basis (e.g. term loan). Regular interest is payable on Debt Finance.

All businesses should have an adequate equity base; if

borrowing is very high, income may not be sufficient to cover interest payments, the lender may call in the debt and the business may crash.

A commonly used criterion for deciding the ratio between Equity and Debt Finance is to calculate whether net trading profits (before interest and tax) will cover interest charges AT LEAST twice over. The main risk in having too much Debt Finance is that income may be insufficient to fund the capital repayments. Much will, however, depend on how efficiently the firm is managed. If, for example, the company is not really maximising its potential earning ability (a transport firm's lorries are only on the road, fully loaded, for 60% of the time), then it would be better to hold more Equity than Debt in the firm's capital structure.

The relationship between Equity finance and Debt Finance is crucial to the survival of a new business, particularly in its early days. Any potential investor will look keenly at this area. A general guideline would be that no investor will wish to invest more money in the business than the proprietor(s).

Once you have calculated the actual figures involved, you can decide on the ratios of Equity Finance and Debt Finance in your enterprise. Be sure to include all capital expenditure (vehicles, machinery, premises, office equipment etc.), wages (staff and yourself/partner), shortfall between income and expenditure (growth in income may be weaker than anticipated).

Your formal Business Plan (see Part Two, Chapter Three), will show a detailed breakdown of the proposed financial structure of the business, but it is useful to keep a broad figure in your head as you think about which potential lender to approach and the general structure of your business. If the amount you need to borrow turns out to be higher than you expected, you may feel that you don't want to be burdened with such a large loan at the outset. Perhaps you could cut costs initially, or rethink your whole business strategy, but NEVER underestimate the potential difference between income and expenditure, especially at the outset.

What can I offer as security?

Every potential lender will ask you what security you can put up to offset the risk he or she will be taking in lending you money, especially if you are asking for a loan. NEVER offer security to a higher value than that of the loan you are taking.

Security can be:

- your home, if you own it outright; or if there is a substantial positive difference between the market value of the property and any outstanding mortgage;

- the business premises, if you own them;

- a life insurance policy; this must be cashable; the insurance company can advise you on this and can tell you the surrender value of your policy;

- a guarantee from a third party that he/she will repay the loan if you are unable to;

- in the case of a company, personal guarantees from the directors that they will repay the debt themselves from their own resources, if the business cannot do so;

- a claim over the assets of the company;

- a life insurance policy to cover the loan if you should die before it is repaid (you will be liable for the premiums on this).

When do I want my business to start?

Many sources of grant aid are impossible to tap into after you have started your business. Make sure that you have thoroughly investigated all likely sources of grants before you commence. You might even find that by modifying your plans or delaying the start of the project slightly that you can qualify for grants you could have otherwise missed. The generation of cash from any possible source in the early stages is critical, and you'd really kick yourself if your impatience were to cost you thousands, or even millions, in grants for which you would have qualified had you waited.

You might even find, by digging deeper, that your main project does not qualify but a part of the business, such as centralized management services or an administration centre, would. By simply modifying the presentation of your proposals you might find help after all.

CASE HISTORY

Company F

Company F was involved in the supply of industrial valves and fittings. The directors thought that there were no grants available. After a review of the company's activity, coupled with an assessment of the possible grant sources, their advisers made a successful application for a Regional Enterprise Grant. The company received £15,000 towards the £100,000 needed to extend the premises and fit them out for an expanded industrial product range.

On the other hand, there are some grants which seem attractive at first, but which carry such onerous burdens as to be not worth having. If you don't do your homework, you might even claim a grant you'll live to regret.

Another important consideration when you are eligible for a grant is your personal or corporate liability to repay the grant if you stop fulfilling the conditions within a given period after receipt.

Once you've bought the machinery or employed the staff, you're unlikely to have that lump sum available again, especially if business slows down to the point of paying off staff or selling machinery. If you have to repay the grant personally it could create a significant problem, and could form part of a substantial claim against your personal assets due to unlimited liability. On the other hand, a limited company is only liable to the value of its shareholders' funds in the company kitty, and in the event of a claim which cannot be met by the company, there is unlikely to be a personal claim against directors, providing they have been fulfilling their duties properly.

Application processes for loans from high street banks are being simplified, apparently, and clients are being told to expect a response within two to five working days of an application being submitted. However, there is normally a great deal of preparation to be done by the applicant before a local manager can submit the paperwork with a reasonable chance of success. Although he or she will probably take notes at your initial meeting, do not expect the manager or anyone else to convert your verbal description into a business plan for you.

Depending on the scale and type of your project, it would be prudent to allow approximately six months to one year for preparation for your business start-up, since it can often take this length of time to prepare sufficient funding to allow the project to commence successfully. If you find that you want or need to get started before you're sure of all funds, you run a very high risk of failure in the early stages of your business development.

POSSIBLE FLOWCHART OF EVENTS

Jan	Feb	Mar	Apr	May	Jun
Write business plan. Raise equity £20,000. Apply for grant.	Agree motor lease finance contract £15,000	Agree machinery finance £15,000.	Bank agrees £15,000 overdraft.	Last holiday before start-up.	Property refit. Term loan agreed £15,000.

Jul	Aug	Sep	Oct	Nov	Dec
Order vehicles (after grant). Grant aid approved £4,500.	Begin refit of property. Pre-sales activity.	Install machinery following factory refit.	Pay bills for refit. Claim grant. Start manu- facture.	Start invoice process.	Grant aid rec'd.

SOURCES OF MONEY
1. Grants
'There is no such thing as a free lunch'

In the real world of small business finance, there are grants which have been dreamed up by some well-meaning bureaucrat or skilful politician, the application process for which is so tortuous and drawn out, and the burdens of acceptance so onerous, that they are simply not worth applying for in certain circumstances.

Don't be fooled by the myth that there are grants freely available for anyone wanting to start a business. Assistance is largely geared towards the creation of jobs by foreign companies bringing inward investment into manufacturing industry. If you look at some of the huge sums handed over to inward investment projects, you'll be tempted to call up your long-lost cousins in far-off places and ask them to be the leading light in your new business, simply to make it look like an investment by a foreign business in the UK. We don't know of specific examples of this, but we could understand why anyone would want to do it!

For the home-grown UK entrepreneur, there are some grants available. Again, they are largely geared towards the creation of jobs in manufacturing, but there is a noticeable interest in biotechnology and computer software engineering. Of less interest to the UK government is the service sector, and so financial incentives for the creation of jobs in distribution, advertising, and other media-related businesses, marketing, the professions etc. are greatly reduced. In the case of retailing (including hotels, shops, hairdressers and other personal services) you'll be lucky to get the merest whiff of encouragement never mind financial aid! (We can't really explain the logic of this to someone who is desperate to open up the best and most innovative hairdressers in town.) However, there are often local sources of financial aid for improving your marketing effort, corporate image, profitability, staff development etc. which can be worth pursuing.

Total finance package of £81,000	
£20,000	own cash
£15,000	leasing or specialist vehicle finance
£15,000	specialist machinery asset finance
£15,000	term loan
£10,000	overdraft
£6,000	grant

In any event, there is no grant available, as far as we are aware, that will provide anyone with 100% of the funds required for any project, whether it be an employee training programme or the purchase of a factory and machinery to start a new manufacturing company. In every case, recipients of grants must show that they are paying their own share. If a company qualifies for 15% of a spend of £100,000, the client still has to find 85% from his/her own resources which can include bank loans. This will be clearer from the table on the previous page showing the structure of a financial package.

£6000 Grant
The grant is 15% of the qualifying expenditure. In this case £20,000 refit costs plus £20,000 for machinery. (Vehicles are not usually eligible for grants.)

£10,000 Working Capital (Bank Overdraft) PLUS £15,000 Bank Term Loan
These are secured by a charge over the firm's free assets (including the sales ledger) and a second charge over the owner/director's home, which is valued at £100,000 with an existing mortgage of £55,000. £15,000 represents 75% of the expenditure on the refitting costs of £20,000.

£15,000 Specialist Machinery Asset Finance
This represents 75% of the £20,000 cost and is provided by

Specialist Asset Financiers. The 25% deposit by the borrower gives a degree of comfort to the lenders. The VAT element of the purchase is met from the overdraft.

£15,000 Specialist Vehicle Finance

This is a similar formula to the Specialist Machinery purchase. In both cases, residual values/re-saleability of the goods provides security.

£20,000 Own Cash

The entrepreneur has used his redundancy money to invest in the new venture. The cash is required as deposits for the above items, plus working capital. This cash, plus the overdraft, is used to fund the VAT element of the expenditure.

2. Bank Loans

Someone once said 'If you've got a £5,000 bank loan and you can't pay it back, you've got a problem. If you've got a £5 million bank loan and you can't pay it back, the bank's got a problem!'.

Banks rarely lend to anyone who desperately needs it, just in case it all goes wrong. They tend to lend money to domestic customers who can show that they don't really need it, but who can demonstrate an ability to repay the sums involved from other sources if the project goes horribly wrong. The reason they do this is because UK banks today need to lend to reliable UK customers who are reasonably financially secure. The banks have lost a considerable amount of money in recent years through lending to unsuitable customers who were unable to repay large loans, and in their own sometimes ill-fated excursions into other areas (such as the property market).

Banks, just like every other source of finance, like to be seen to be the most important part of your financial jigsaw. This usually means that you have to show your chosen potential lender that everybody financially involved has already agreed to go ahead, and that now you are only waiting for the bank (or whoever happens to be your target) to give it the go-ahead by joining in. If the bank manager seems reluctant to commit hard cash to your project, and you have decided that the bank is your best option for money, then you can try dropping the hint that there is another direct competitor currently considering their financial involvement, and whose positive decision is imminent. Of course this has to be true and you will already have been discussing the matter with one or more competitive sources. This might just galvanize the bank manager into decisive action in your favour. The two most common types of bank loans that you will come across are:

(a) Overdraft

(b) Term Loan

It may be possible to negotiate a fixed rate of interest for the period of the loan, to avoid the uncertainty of possible variations in interest rates. You will find, however, that banks demand a rate which may be substantially higher than their variable rate, if rates are relatively low. If there is not much difference between variable and fixed rates offered (when rates are relatively high) this probably indicates that rates are expected to fall soon, or at least remain stable.

Overdraft

Although overdrafts are commonly used by businesses, they can be potentially dangerous for expanding enterprises whose levels of security are already fully utilized by the bank. Overdrafts are repayable ON DEMAND if the bank thinks your project is faltering. Because your house, flat or other main residence is likely to be the chief security for this, you run the risk of losing the lot if you get your business sums wrong!

Term Loan

We believe that this is the preferred method of borrowing in some other European countries, such as Germany, where overdrafts are less favoured. It provides a lump sum for agreed business purposes, with both capital and interest being repaid over a specified period. Since it cannot normally be recalled at the whim of the bank unless the borrower is in default of payments, it provides a degree of peace of mind for the faithful borrower.

In the UK, these loans are usually associated with the purchase of property or equipment, and normally repayable over a period of 3-20 years, to suit the useful life of the purchase, which is also the main security for the loan.

Loans are generally made at variable rates of interest, with lending limit of 60-80% of the purchase price of the asset, subject to the borrower's ability to repay.

Sometimes, when a company or firm has a more or less permanent overdraft, a bank will agree to convert some or all of it to a term loan, in order to create a more ordered method of paying it off. This tends to lend weight to the argument for continental-style term lending for business in certain circumstances. Of course, each case is different, borrowing requirements can vary dramatically for similar businesses, and each is considered on its own merits.

3. Factoring

This is an interesting possibility, especially for anyone manufacturing a product for sale to business, not to private individuals, (e.g. roof trusses for construction), or to firms providing a clearly measurable and definable service, such as plant hire.

Factors are normally specialised lending subsidiaries of banks, and, by having your sales invoices 'assigned' to them, they effectively lend you a percentage of your sales in advance of the client actually settling their bill. The great thing is, providing your invoices are genuinely collectable, you do not normally have to provide any personal security, as the factoring company considers your sales ledger and clients' respectability to be adequate security for the money advanced.

There is a charge for the amount of money advanced, broadly similar to the cost of an overdraft, and there is also a management charge levied for taking over the management of your sales ledger and credit control. In many cases this can be offset by savings in avoiding bad debt risks, since the factoring firm will advise you on the credit rating of existing or potential clients, and will generally be more skilful in calling in late payments which might otherwise never be paid.

CASE HISTORY
Company K

Company K was involved in scaffold contracting and hire, with a clientele of long-established, publicly listed construction firms, local authorities and small- to medium-sized builders. Due to the success of recent tendering for work, the company needed approximately £25,000 extra working capital for the day-to-day running of the business. Discussions with the bank followed, and the bank intimated that a facility of £25,000 could be made available. However, since the bank viewed scaffolding equipment as inadequate security for the loan, it would require the directors to provide the following information:

1. Up-to-date management accounts.
2. Full statements of the personal means of all the directors.
3. Full statements of the personal means of all directors' spouses.
4. Complete breakdowns of monthly domestic income for all directors and spouses.
5. Personal guarantees of each director for the sum in question.
6. Where possible, a charge over the personal home of each director.
7. A charge over the free assets of the company.

The directors felt that the bank was asking for too much by way of personal information from spouses, in particular, and for too much by way of security over personal assets in relation to the relatively small sum involved. Furthermore, this would have meant that it would have proved almost impossible to persuade the bank to lend more in the future, as all possible security would have already been committed to this initial loan.

In this case, the alternative of factoring was found to be more attractive. The factoring company advanced the amount requested, secured against only the value of the outstanding sales ledger. In addition, this method of financing meant that if a further opportunity cropped up, a facility to borrow up to £50,000 in total on the strength of the existing sales ledger was already in position.

On a personal basis, the directors also had no need to divulge unnecessary details of their personal means and spouses' income and assets.

It's a great concept if it suits your business, but a lot of preparation is necessary in advance and it's not the solution to every problem.

4. Partners (as a source of finance)

See Chapter One of this section for information on the financial implications of partnerships.

5. Investors

If you only have a little of your own money with which to start your business and you feel that your marvellous idea's money-making potential will prove irresistible to others, you could try several routes to raising outside investment.

Private Investors

To make investment in new or expanding companies more attractive, the government has put in place a scheme which has certain tax advantages for investors, subject to conditions. The current scheme is known as the *Enterprise Investment Scheme*, or EIS. Broadly speaking, an outside investor taking less than 30% of the ordinary shares in a Private or non-quoted Public Limited Company can qualify for the following tax benefits:

- Tax rebate of up to 20% of the sum invested, up to £100,000 per anum per person (investment);

- Roll-over relief on capital gains equivalent to the sum invested (your accountant can explain this);

- Tax-free profit (capital gain) on the disposal of shares after a qualifying period of five years has elapsed.

If a business will carry out a qualifying activity within EIS guidelines, the above benefits can either:

- Help turn your ordinary profits into extra-special returns;

- Compensate for lack of performance in the early stages of business development, providing what might be considered a normal return on investments, thanks to the tax breaks available.

- If the worst comes to the worst any capital losses sustained by investors can be deducted from tax bills.

There are private investors who don't want to get too involved over a five year period, and who might prefer a quicker exit. In any case, if you find out that your business will qualify for EIS tax relief, it is worth putting the paperwork in place as an attractive option.

You or your family can qualify for tax relief if you plan it properly. The other advantage for you in doing so is that you will be showing potential lenders and investors that:

- You have made a thorough job of researching your project from all angles;

- You have the best interests of your backers at heart.

Your accountant or bank manager could possibly advise you on whether you may qualify for the scheme, but this is a specialist area. Your local tax office can certainly provide further details.

Institutions

Investment managers have millions, or even billions, of pounds available for investment in potentially profitable ventures. From a small business perspective, these are often unavailable, since the minimum available for investment can be far in excess of what is required or justifiable, and can be equivalent to several years' projected turnover!

Institutions as potential investors are worth bearing in mind, however, particularly once the company has been going strongly for a couple of years.

Venture Capitalists

It can come as a shock to the would-be entrepreneur looking to raise £50,000 that this is likely to be the minimum CHARGE made by a venture capital firm, rather than the amount it would invest! It has been commented recently that there is no one less adventurous than an established venture capitalist. The sums available are huge, but they are looking for what they consider to be relatively safe and stable investments, such as a management buy-out (MBO) from an established firm or group or a management buy-in (MBI) by an external team of experienced managers. Minimum investments tend to be around £1 million despite claims to the contrary by many firms, but there are some smaller specialist investors who might go as low (!) as £500,000 or even £250,000. The charges made are high to compensate for the perceived risk of the sector.

In recognition of this gap in the market, some new schemes have been initiated. These try to act as 'marriage bureaux', bringing together investors and investees, often screening applicants in the initial stages. One UK-wide operation is the Local Investment Networking Company (LINC). Others can be found advertising in the *Financial Times* or in the business pages of your local and regional newspapers.

CASE HISTORY
Company P

Having read the British Venture Capital Association's yearbook, company P identified over 20 firms claiming to seek the opportunity to invest sums from £500,000. The company approached these potential investors and received replies stating that either the amount or the industry sector involved was not of interest to these firms. Finally company P found a specialist investor who was operating at the level necessary, and approaches were made. Following an initial presentation of the business plan, adjustments and modifications were made to suit the investor, and the investor made a verbal commitment three months later.

By this time the directors had found a trade supplier who would offer extended credit over 18 months, using the value of goods supplied as his security, but only for 50% of the amount originally sought. This was felt to be more attractive than the venture capitalist company's offer, so the directors scaled down the size of the project and happily clinched the deal.

Family and Friends

Many people shy away from borrowing, or taking investment, from members of their own family and their friends. This is understandable, since who wants to be responsible for losing their money and be turned into a pariah?

However the old proverb 'many hands make light work' can be

applied here. If you believe that your idea stands more than a fair chance of success, can show impartiality, and provide sound supporting information to back you up, you could use something like the EIS scheme to structure an investment for family and friends, to be regarded as in much the same way as a 'bit of a flutter'. You should encourage them to treat their investment like putting money on an outsider in the Grand National or buying a handful of lottery tickets every week – fantastic fun if they've backed a real winner, with a lucky windfall, or nothing at all back if it goes wrong. In other words they should only put in as much as they can afford to lose. You might think that this is a bit of a negative approach, since you are convinced of the merits of your proposal, but not everyone gets as lucky as the gentleman who backed Anita and Gordon Roddick in the early days of the Body Shop: his initial £4000 invested became worth tens of millions of pounds! Rally the troops, however, and spread the risk.

Own funds
This source has been deliberately left to the end of this section, and with good reason.
It would be unusual for any business to get off the ground without some financial commitment from the entrepreneur himself, and one of the easiest traps to fall into is to finance all the early stages of development from your own funds, only to find that further finance from other sources is urgently required, either to complete the initial stage or to move onto an intermediate stage.

If you fall into this trap, it will be a frustrating experience and a bitter lesson. If you go to a bank or other investors and your own pockets are by now empty, you are in some ways showing them how incredibly naive you have been in going off only half prepared. Banks will not be impressed, and Venture Capitalists are unlikely to want to know you. Your precious business idea can suddenly fall prey to 'Vulture Capitalists'. They will circle round your business like the lame animal it has now become, waiting for the right moment to strike and carry it off into their own lair to be dissected and devoured at their leisure, with precious little left over for you. If you're lucky you'll meet a sympathetic soul, but don't count on it.

By planning carefully, and not commencing business until all the financial sources have been investigated fully, not only do you keep your options open for possible grant aid, you hang onto one of your most valuable assets at this stage – CASH!

REMEMBER – CASH IS KING!

Wherever possible, try to get investors, suppliers of grant sources and lenders to share the financial risks at every stage of the development of your business, always keeping some of your own cash in reserve for that unforeseen emergency, or for the cash contribution which will be required for other parties to look favourably upon financing the next stage. Should the unthinkable happen, and the business fail at any stage, you have a sufficient buffer of cash to help you and your family survive any drastic drop in income.

3. WRITING THE BUSINESS PLAN

Recapitulation

Before you begin this mammoth exercise, pause again and reconsider your plans, realistically and honestly. Ask yourself if you have really thought it all through yet. You might be about to embark upon one of the most thrilling and rewarding adventures of your life, or one of the most disastrous. It's easy to think that people in business for themselves always get it right, and have a marvellous lifestyle, jetting around the world in their private aeroplanes after a couple of years hard work. The reality is that most people who are in business are ordinary folk like you and me who put in longer days than they would in a 'normal' job, often for less net income than they would earn on a pro-rata basis per hour worked! There are, of course, many people whose business gives them an income and lifestyle which would otherwise have been out of reach for them in employment, and we all hope that budding entrepreneurs eventually earn what they deserve from their business for all the hard work and effort that they'll put in.

You will find, in discussion with other like-minded people, especially if they have been in business for a while with a degree of success, that there are other benefits of being in business which carry more weight than mere money. Freedom, control, independence, responsibility and self-satisfaction are among the benefits which are likely to be rated most highly.

Despite the adverse experiences of business encountered by around 99.9% of all those brave or mad enough to have gone down the independent route, you will find it difficult to find many who would say that they regretted doing so. However, you will certainly find a substantial proportion who would readily admit that they would have done it differently, if they had known then what they know now!

That, in essence, is what we are trying to capture for your benefit. If the distilled experiences of people who have done it all the hard way can be learned in principle from this book, then the reader is already a step ahead of those who think that they know it all. But no matter how much you read about it, there is nothing which can prepare you 100% for the real thing. Our hope is that the information contained in this book will help you to hone your natural instincts for survival in the business jungle. So before you go any further, just pause for a moment and ask yourself:

Is this really what I want?
Am I willing to take the risk?
Am I up to it?

If the answer is 'Yes!' to all three questions, then press on with your project. For most people the next step will be the preparation of the detailed Business Plan in order to raise the money to get started.

Writing your Business Plan

You have now had a chance to think about the key factors which will affect your decision to go into business, and to compare your idea as it developed with the original concept. You are more familiar with the less positive aspects of being in business than you were before you began reading this book, and you are ready in part to cope with some possible adverse circumstances should they arise. You should be able to use this knowledge to allow you to prepare a detailed and well-structured Business Plan which will allow you to illustrate your ability to cope, and to raise the necessary finance to get the business off the ground and developed into an efficient commercial machine. If you have prepared your Personal Summary and the Outline Business Plan as suggested earlier in the book, then you will already have ordered your thoughts, planned your business strategy and set them down on paper. Now you can use these as bases for the in-depth analysis of your project expressed in the Business Plan, and the Supporting Information which will be attached to the document as Appendices.

Think of your Business Plan as a sales document. In selling, there is an accepted method of getting your message across, and this lends itself to the structure of a Business Plan. It is as follows:

Tell them what you're going to tell them
Tell them
Tell them what you've told them

You are going to use this technique to persuade someone, probably a bank, to BUY your idea in principle. To do so, you must illustrate that what you have to offer them is a good match for their buying criteria – in other words it gives them what they want. Of course to do this, you need to know what they want first. What would be the point of sending out possibly dozens of copies to people unless you were sure that it contained a proposition that was in some way useful to them? We all know that banks are in business to borrow (from depositors and savers) and lend (to housebuyers and businesses, for example) money. Do not imagine for one second, however, that just because you've got what you consider to be a fabulous business idea, the banks will be falling over themselves to lend to YOU. Not a bit of it. It's more like a game where the bank manager sits there, holding an enormous sack of cash in his hand, but just out of your reach across the desk, saying:

'I've got loads of money here, but you're not getting any of it. Why should I let you get your hands on it, when I can lend it to other people with very little risk at all. So, what are you going to do about it?'

Your task is to understand what the lender wants and write such a marvellously convincing (and true) story that he is persuaded to give up the security of lending to others and give you some funds to start your own business. To do so you will have to illustrate that, for example:

- your business is in an industry which is worthy of his investment;
- you have a clear idea of the business which you want to be in and the cost of doing so;
- you have the personal experience and necessary support team to be succesful;
- you have fully researched the market and pre-sold your ideas to clients where possible;
- you can repay from the profits of the business the amount borrowed in a reasonable time-span;
- you can earn him an adequate return on the loan;
- you can offer security for the loan as an alternative means of getting the bank's money back.

If you can achieve all of the above, you should be able to get the loan you require.

By using the general format provided, your business plan can be adapted where necessary to meet the presentation requirements of most potential sources of finance. Make sure that you ask your accountant or other adviser to read through the plan before you use it, and incorporate any useful suggestions which they might make. You might even find that your accountant will be only too happy to assist with the financial projections element of your business plan, and tidy up the wording, for a fee which is substantially less than that which they would have charged had they been asked to produce the entire plan from scratch. From a bank manager or other lender's point of view it is a plus point if you can show that your accountant has been involved in thinking through the figures in some detail.

> In some cases grants may be available to assist with accountants' fees in the setting up of a business.

You will have done most of the hard work in the preparation of your Business Plan. It is far easier for someone else to criticize constructively when they have not had to do all the hard research, soul-searching, foot-slogging and writing that was necessary to put it together. When inviting comment and constructive criticism, do not take it personally if you find that your presentation is not understood by the reader. This should be a warning to you that you have used language or jargon that is not easily understood, or that the structure of your argument is not all it could be.

Structure of the Business Plan

The length of a business plan will depend on various factors, especially the amount of money which you are trying to raise, and the amount of technical detail necessary to satisfy the lenders or other participants involved. But whether the plan is short or long, it will help you if you use the following structure. There are essentially five parts:

1. Executive Summary (one page)
2. The Story

3. The Financial Data
4. Closing Summary
5. Appendices (Supporting Information)

Let us now expand these areas in some detail.

1. Executive Summary

This is akin to the summary of papers presented to a Government Minister by his Personal Private Secretary. The relevant detail is presented in a quickly readable and easily understood format, and the Minister can simply rubberstamp the item based on a condensed knowledge of the matter, knowing that it has been thoroughly researched, and that there is supporting information in the file. Your Executive Summary explains your plans, should inspire confidence in the bank manager and be easily understood while allowing him or her the opportunity to ask searching questions. The answers to these questions will, of course, have been fully covered in the plan proper, and you can refer the manager to the relevant pages. The Executive Summary should contain sufficient information on your business proposals to give someone with no experience of your industry a fairly broad but clear and concise idea of

what you intend to do
why you intend to do this
how you intend to do it

Your Personal Summary and the Introduction section of your Outline Business Plan will provide you with most of the information you need here.

2. The Story

Never underestimate the value of the narrative part of your business plan. If you think this is an exaggeration, ask yourself why some shares quoted on the stock exchange change hands at prices (in terms of multiples of earnings) far higher than those of comparable rivals. It's all down to the STORY, of course, which accompanies the bare figures. Usually investors in the stock market are hoping for some breakthrough or specialist innovation which can lead to super profits in the future, either through increased competitiveness, market share or even a buy-out by another company looking for a goose to lay some golden eggs for it. The story told by the company has to be truthful, of course, but an upbeat story encourages optimism and attracts investors. Remember, there is only one thing more infectious than enthusiasm, and that's the LACK of it!

This is your opportunity to tell the world all about your marvellous business idea and the possibilities which will be created by it. You might feel that your literary skills are not quite up to this, in which case employ someone like your accountant to create his version of your story from the verbal and written information which you can provide. Bear in mind that it might not be as flowery and eloquent as you might have made it, but it gets the job done, and in a recognizable format.

Just make sure that the optimist rather than the pessimist in him is allowed to shine through! The added benefit in this is that your accountant will tend to speak the same language as your bank manager, and will therefore express your intentions in terms which are, for him,'user friendly': make sure that you understand it yourself, though, otherwise it could lead to a potentially embarrassing interview when you are asked questions by your bank manager in a language which you may find to be alien. The Business Strategy, Management and Marketing Sections of your Outline Business Plan will help you here.

There are five principal areas you should consider tackling when composing the story:

1. The Business Opportunity
2. The Management Team
3. The Market
4. The Unique Selling Point
5. The Company Image

1. The Business Opportunity
This section gives you the chance to present your project as a viable business opportunity; you can show why you believe in its potential and support your argument as follows (where appropriate):

Give a detailed analysis of your product/service;

Show what opportunity exists for your business and why you
   believe in this opportunity;
Describe what advantages your product/service has over its
   competitors;
Outline your sales strategy and pricing policy;
Indicate who will be your customers;
State where the business will operate from;
Indicate when you will be in a position to start;
Show how you see your business developing.

The Business Strategy Section of your Outline Business Plan
will provide the basic information you need here and you can
expand on this. Use photographs, diagrams and sketches
where possible to make it easier for the reader to get an idea of
what you are describing. You should also include a brief
summary of your curriculum vitae (CV) stating your age,
qualifications and recent relevant experience of the industry in
which you intend to operate your business. Do not elaborate in
areas that are not relevant to the business. (A full CV should be
given in the Supporting Information section (as an Appendix)
and include your full home address).

2. The Management Team

The Management Section of your Outline Business Plan will
form the basis of this section and we suggest you consider
expanding on the following points where appropriate.

If your business idea is fairly small-scale and suited to a 'one man' or 'one woman' structure (e.g. chauffeuring, photography, freelance word-processing, driving instruction, gardening, clock repairs), you will have to show the potential lender that you can take care of the day-to-day management of the business – or that you are prepared to pay for someone to do this for you. We have frequently emphasized in this book that poor management has been the downfall of many a potentially successful business, and this applies to the smaller as well as the larger operation. Lenders are well aware of the need for good management and will be particularly interested in your planned accounting procedures; they will not be impressed by vague promises or attempts to fudge the issue.

If your business involves two or more people, then you must set out clearly the areas of responsibility. Banks don't like lending to 'one-man bands', i.e. businesses which can be paralysed by the owner/manager's lack of ability to delegate responsibility.

You will need to satisfy the lender (if you can) that not only do you have knowledge and experience of the industry, but you have also the maturity to recruit managers, advisers or a board of directors with the depth of experience to make sure that this business will not come off the rails if you disappear, either temporarily or permanently. If you need full-time employees as members of your management, make sure that they are of a sufficient level of competence in their field to bolster your management strengths and bring complementary skills which will assist you and your business. Employ the best you can afford, not the cheapest you can get.

Show the lender that the members of the team each have their own areas of specific responsibility, and are able to assist each other from time to time, especially when holidays or sickness cause interruptions.

Provide:

- a breakdown of titles and responsibilities;
- an organization chart to show how responsibility will be shared by the members of the team;
- a summary of the team's recent relevant experience, along with details of any other relevant business interests, directorships and shareholdings.

Include a full CV for each member of the management team in the Appendix for this section, to include the full home addresses of all directors.

Don't be afraid to approach some of the better-known members of the local business community who might have recently retired or be about to retire, to ask them if they could spare a few hours per month in an advisory or non-executive capacity. The wealth of knowledge which they can bring, along with their lifelong network of contacts will be well worth the expense if you can afford it, and their comforting presence will be appreciated by any lender. Your accountant might be able to advise on the likely cost of this.

If there are members of staff in addition to the management team, it would be useful to provide a breakdown of the number and type of staff that will be necessary to operate the business.

Having gone to so much trouble to build an efficient management team, it might well be advisable to show that you intend to insure not only them but yourself against the perils of critical illness, incapacity or death, to ensure that the business can survive the lack of any of its key personnel.

Where certain services are to be provided on a contract basis from a third party, such as book-keeping or telephone answering (for example, if you use a business centre with this service), remember to note this in the plan too, to show that you have taken the requirement and costs into consideration.

3. The Market

This is a very important part of your Business Plan and is your opportunity to convince the potential lender that your idea is not just a slice of 'pie in the sky' but a sound, solid business opportunity. In the Marketing section of your Outline Business Plan you demonstrated that you were convinced of the potential demand for your product or service, that you understood how to market it and that you believed in its potential. Here you can reiterate your convictions but more detail is required to show the lender, who may be sceptical about your optimism, that you can provide facts and figures to back up your claims. It is impossible to give a precise guide on how to do this for every budding entrepreneur reading this book as every different type of business will require a different approach. Broadly, however, every lender needs to know that you have taken the time and trouble to research the demand for your product or service and can provide hard evidence to back up your conclusion that there is a clear demand for it. So where do you start? Perhaps the easiest way of thinking about it is to look at your target market and ask yourself

Who will be my customers?
What do they want to buy?
Where do they buy it at the moment?
How much do they pay for it now?
Why will they buy my product or service instead?

The answers to these questions will provide you with supporting information for your argument. Try to express as much information as possible in figures – the more figures you can produce, the more authoritative your plan will appear.

4. The Unique Selling Point

Highlight the unique selling point of your business. If you don't know what it is yet, you'd better give it some thought: your unique selling point is that aspect of your product or service that makes you stand out from the competition, and which is particular and unique to you. It could be, for example, your location if you're the only one in town, or a range of colours offered, or quality of service. You will have one – or possibly more – selling points and each will be instrumental in encouraging the lender to support you.

Be very careful about using a lower price than your competitors as your selling point; cheapness is not always best. People buy products and services for all kinds of reasons, rational and irrational, of which price is only one.

---

5. The Company Image

What position in the market do you wish to adopt? How will you represent your company? What will be your image (e.g. cheap and cheerful or expensive and luxurious)?

Now that you have decided on your target market, unique selling point and company Image you will need some facts and figures to back up your claims. As a general rule, provide as many relevant facts and figures as you can in your Appendix to this section, to add weight to your arguments. Don't be put off by the idea of 'research' – it really isn't that difficult. There are various ways of conducting research, but they all come down to the two principal methods, *desk research* and *original research*.

Desk research can include reading newspapers, magazines, market research surveys and advertisements. Market research reports from industry sources can be quoted and referred to; these can be found in the business section of the larger public libraries and the nearest Chamber of Commerce may be able to help. Most libraries have photocopying facilities for reference books, so you can photocopy tables, diagrams etc.

Original research generally means getting out and about and doing your own market research! Visit potential customers, retailers, distributors – everyone who might be associated with your new business. Ask them what they're looking for and what they like/dislike about their current suppliers. You can also visit potential competitors – you are unlikely to be challenged as a potential rival. Collect brochures, leaflets, price-lists.

The final part of this section should include an indication of how you plan to penetrate the chosen market and get your business off the ground. Indicate what kind of advertising campaign you have chosen, together with likely costs.

The marketing part of your story is crucial to the Business Plan. It is your opportunity to show the lender that you have 'done your homework', are informed, prepared and businesslike. In conclusion, therefore, the main body of your text should demonstrate clearly that:

- there is a demand for your product or service (backed up by the results of your market research; summarize in the main body of the text, but include figures, tables etc. in the Appendix to this section);

91

- you have identified a niche which your company can fill with its attributes (again with supporting information in the Appendix)

- you have evaluated the competition;

- you have decided how best to penetrate the market.

For further help on marketing, turn to Part Three, Chapter One, *Marketing and Selling*. Here the principles of marketing are outlined and more detailed help is given.

3. The Financial Data

You will already have given some considerable thought to the financial aspects of your intended enterprise in the Principal Risks and Finance sections of your Outline Business Plan. Now it is time to cover these areas in greater depth. Firstly, ask yourself the three Key Questions:

How much money do I need?
How much have I got?
Where can I get the rest?

It may seem obvious to you that you should have your finances sorted out before starting your business, but you would be amazed at the number of businesses which are set up on the most precarious of financial footings. These, however, are the businesses which have the greatest likelihood of failure in the early stages due to what is commonly referred to as undercapitalization.

You will find that if you are currently 'resting' between leaving your last job and setting up your business, the act of raising finance is all the more difficult. If at all possible, avoid becoming unemployed as this will lower your credit rating in the eyes of potential lenders unless you have a substantial cash pile to fall back on. This is especially important for those of you who will operate as sole traders or partners and who have a need for loans to get started. If you have the opportunity to be employed, even on a temporary basis, until you are ready to launch your business proper, take it, especially in the field in which you intend to operate independently. Think about this practical point: would you lend money to someone who is unemployed, with no track record and no guarantee of income to pay back the loan?

This means that there were insufficient funds available to the business to cope with either:

Business turnover lower than expectations – cash reserves used up in paying bills, loan interest etc. and funds running out before the business was firmly established

or

Business turnover higher than expectations – cash used up buying in unexpectedly high quantities of materials etc. before money starts to come in quickly enough from trading.

93

This is also referred to as overtrading (some would say running before you can walk or biting off more than you can chew).

Sadly, there are a great many businesses which have failed through being unable to fund the early stages of development. Had an adequate financial package been in place at the appropriate time, many would have become established and successful in their field, providing the owners with the lifestyle they wanted and their employees with jobs.

A necessary part of your business plan is of course your cash flow forecast and profit and loss projections. In order to estimate or calculate how cash will flow in and out of your business, you will have to ask yourself these questions:

- How much would it cost to buy all the fixtures and fittings and equipment I need to get started?
- What possible ways are there to finance these purchases?
- What will be the cost of initial stock, stationery and other consumable items I need?
- How long will it be before I have to pay for these?
- How much money will I need to spend on everyday expenses like insurance, wages, vehicles, electricity, gas, rent and rates before I get any revenue?
- When are these payments due to be made, and can I set up a payment plan to suit my cash flow?

Clearly, there are many areas which you will have to consider on an individual basis before you can arrive at an approximation of cash flow. When putting together your financial package it is also critical that you take into account the cost of borrowed money. Interest charges will be made on a regular basis, usually every month or every three months, depending on the type of loan. Of course, until you have a rough idea of the types of loan available to you, it will be difficult to work out the cost of repayments. A useful exercise would be to contact your local bank, enterprise trust or equivalent organization and explain to the manager or adviser that you are beginning to put your business plan together and need some advice regarding the various types of finance possibly available to you.

Firstly we will look at some of the major issues involved in planning an appropriate financial package for your enterprise, and secondly we look at how to put together a cash flow forecast followed by a sample layout to help you.

1. Structuring the Financial Package.

To the uninitiated entrepreneur, raising finance for a business may seem quite simple. Surely all one has to do is pop one's head round the manager's door while next at the bank, and offer to discuss, there and then over tea and biscuits, how much one will allow the bank to lend one to set up this marvellously profitable new venture? Sketch a quick outline on the old boy's desk-top blotting pad to make sure he doesn't forget how the business to be the envy of all businesses will be able to accumulate vast wealth quicker than the bank can lend anyway, once things start to roll, of course! Then it's off one goes with a cheery wave to collect the new car from the Jaguar dealer's showroom, a fat cheque protruding from one's top pocket at a jaunty angle.

Unfortunately, in most cases, nothing could be further from the truth.

It may come as a shock to learn this, but contrary to popular belief, it can be extremely difficult to persuade anyone to provide finance for a small business, particularly a new start. When considering lending, banks and others will want to see some sort of track record of the potential borrower, and a strongly argued case has to be presented if there is to be any hope of success. Indeed, many entrepreneurs who have managed to raise the money to get started will confirm that securing the finance was actually the hardest part of all. This is why the budding entrepreneur will need vast reserves of enthusiasm, determination and tenacity. If you can raise the money, you will have convinced a team of professional sceptics, against almost overwhelming odds, that you have what it takes to succeed in business.

In addition to proving that you have the necessary experience to manage such an enterprise, you will be expected to show that you are personally committed to the success of this venture. If you think about it from a lender's perspective, you are asking someone (who in all probability doesn't know you from Adam) to place a bet on you to the tune of several thousand pounds, in the hope that you'll be as good as you say you are. Their reward for this magnanimous gesture will be a paltry percentage interest every year until the loan is repaid in full. Put yourself in their position for a moment: does this seem like the deal of a lifetime? Of course it doesn't. They've probably heard it all before. If you were in their shoes, and presented with the opportunity to invest in this would-be entrepreneur and his or her risky business, you'd probably run a country mile at the prospect. This is why it is essential to understand what lenders, investors and grant-awarding bodies will stipulate as their specific criteria, and what it is that will provide comfort for them and attract them to your proposal.

These criteria can include:

1. Stage of Business Development: Pre-Start-up or Recently Started
2. Industry type
3. Business type/sector of operation
4. Business structure: your personal financial involvement
5. Financial controls
6. Financial partners
7. Customers
8. Suppliers
9. Security (collateral within and outwith the business)

In carefully considering each of these points we can begin to identify probable or possible sources of finance.

1. Stage of Business Development

Broadly speaking, we expect the readers of this book to fall into either the Pre-Start-up or the Recently Started category.

Pre-Start-up

The Pre-Start-up stage is almost certainly the better one of the two for the following reasons:

- You have not yet passed the point of no return, and can therefore make adjustments to accommodate potential lenders/investors relatively painlessly;

- You still have a degree of independence, and do not necessarily have to take the first or indeed any offer of finance;

- You are in a position of relative strength for negotiating terms with potential backers;

- Hopefully you still have most of your own cash in reserve to show your tangible willingness to 'put your money where your mouth is';

- Crucially, you are still eligible for certain important grants for which you or your business might qualify;

- You may also still have possible alternative employment or income.

If your negotiations lead nowhere or you decide that the financial backing available would be insufficient for a successful start-up, you can shelve the idea until the time is right.

Recently Started

If you have already begun your business in the hope that appropriate financing will be secured as you go along, you have already lost a degree of control over your own business. You may have put yourself in a weaker negotiating position, and will probably need the money more urgently than anticipated in order to meet supply deadlines, unexpected shortfalls in business revenues or other unforeseen problems.

Certain grants for new businesses (e.g. the Enterprise Allowance) are only available if you apply in advance of starting up. Other discretionary grants (e.g. Regional Selective Assistance) could be available if you can show that the project could not succeed or start without the assistance of these funds. If you set off too soon you might have automatically disqualified yourself from this possibility, and at the same time exposed yourself to the risk which they are specifically designed to help you avoid.

However, both categories suffer from the fact that there is little or no track record, and you probably have little to offer lenders by way of collateral in the business as security for a loan. This makes it extremely hard to raise finance from banks, finance houses etc. except possibly where vehicles or other large items of equipment are being purchased, and where the asset itself is easily identifiable (vans, printing machinery) and is acceptable security (collateral) for the loan being provided. On the other hand, the banks in particular are only likely to lend against further collateral as security. If you already have considerable equity in your home or a valuable portfolio of publicly traded stocks and shares, then they will probably fall over themselves to lend you the money.

Borrow early and repay on time

Lenders are not in business to do you any favours. They will make a decision to lend based on hard fact, experience, attractiveness and likely profitability of the loan. If you are fortunate enough to have a proposition which is attractive to more than one possible lender, you will probably find that this will bring out the competitive animal in them. Use this to your advantage to negotiate the best rate you can, or if possible split the loan in order to build up a track record with more than one lender. You will almost certainly need finance again at some point in the future for your ambitious expansion, and the fact that you have two or more parties who have had favourable dealings with you will be to your advantage.

If you have not yet left your employment to start your business, you will find it infinitely easier to borrow money NOW for a car or van which you will then be able to use in your future business, since you are still in receipt of steady income and can get the usual employers' references. Make sure that you have all that you will need for the foreseeable future in the way of major personal borrowings in place (e.g. mortgage) before starting your business. It can be very disheartening to find that YOU can't get a mortgage as easily as your staff once you've taken the plunge. Be aware, however, that these debts have to be kept to manageable proportions, because you will have to be certain that you can continue to make the agreed payments once you have become independent, otherwise you risk losing everything by having it repossessed.

There is a strange anomaly which makes the employees of a sole trader appear to be better credit risks than their employer. Bear this in mind when starting your business, and don't be surprised to find that your staff can get interest-free credit on their new hi-fi more easily than you can in the early days. In some circumstances it can be a real disadvantage to be a fledgling entrepreneur. Unfortunately, when it comes to residential mortgages, you are likely to be shunned by most lenders until you have built up a decent track record in business. Normally, lenders will ask to see three years' accounts, to allow them to judge your performance. In addition, you will be asked to provide projections for the next two years.

This leads us to another problem, which is that you are likely to operate your business in such a way as to legitimately minimize your tax liability. For example, if you have a spouse or live-in partner who does not work elsewhere, you could split one highly-taxable income of £40,000 into two incomes of £20,000, which would, individually, attract less income tax. As you would expect, this is completely at odds with what your bankers and other lenders want, since they might view your perfectly understandable tax-minimizing activity as poor commercial performance.

2. Industry Type

Lenders or investors tend to follow the herd. If the property industry is unpopular with one lender, it's probably unpopular with most of them. You will no doubt remember how the banks were extremely keen to lend for residential mortgages in the eighties, helping to fuel the property price boom that swept the country. Towards the end of the eighties, property became a dirty word as prices crashed in London and the south-east of the country. This price crash did not happen in other areas of Britain, but those areas were still affected as banks sent messages out to branches throughout the country to stop lending on property. Businesses which had substantial or even modest portfolios were asked to reduce the amount of borrowing in order to reduce the banks' exposure. This put needless pressure on the cash flow of many businesses which were healthy, and this in itself caused certain problems of liquidity for the clients while minimizing the risk to the banks.

Other industries might prove to be more popular with venture capitalists than with banks, thanks to a historic or recent spate of spectacular successes. One example is the mobile telephone industry, where many millions of pounds have been invested thanks to the fabulous returns that have been seen to be earned by certain speculative investors as the market now matures and stabilizes, and companies' shares are being floated on the stock exchange.

If your chosen area of operation is in vogue, then you're in luck. Remember, however, that small businesses are less popular than big businesses. Look carefully at the scale of what you're trying to do. Take professional advice and talk to the experts about how best to develop your idea.

3. Business Type/Sector of Operation

You may have chosen an industry which is not so fashionable with investors, nor popular with high-street banks. Such an area might be the construction industry, which is perceived as being high-risk and not for the faint-hearted. However, within that industry there will be certain specialist sectors which can attract funding from alternative sources.

The funding of contract scaffolding for example does not appeal to banks as being an attractive lending proposition. As a sub-contractor, the scaffolding contractor runs the risk of delayed payment or non-payment from his client, the main contractor on the site. In order for a high-street bank to be tempted to lend money to such a venture, it will seek additional security for the loan, such as a personal guarantee plus a second charge over the private home the directors or proprietors to provide additional security.

However, in certain circumstances it is possible to find a specialist lender such as a factoring company which will effectively advance up to 75% of the money tied up in sales invoices. The factoring company actually 'buys' the invoices from the company issuing the invoices, then takes over the management of the sales ledger and works with its client to operate an effective system of credit control. Personal guarantees are not usually required, and there is no need for directors to put their home up as security for this type of facility.

Factoring can replace the need for an overdraft, or work in addition to it, providing both bank and factoring company are happy with the arrangement.

You may have chosen a sector which could prove popular with specialist lenders, but you will need to do your research thoroughly. See Chapter Two of this section for additional information on Factoring.

4. Business Structure: your personal financial involvement
In Part Two, Chapter One, we outlined the various ways a business can be organized. Any lender will be keen to know what kind of status you envisage for your enterprise, and to

what extent they can call upon you to make good any financial deficiency from your own personal reserves.

If you plan to keep your home out of the picture as far as business is concerned, and not have it put at risk in any way, pay particular attention to this section.

If you are a sole trader or partner and you have business loans, then your home, if your name is on the title deeds as owner, is at risk. In the event of non-payment of commercial debts (loans and trade debts) by the business, all your personal assets become fair game for the creditors. Of course, this may never happen, but you might feel a bit more relaxed if you knew your family home was sacrosanct. If you can show the bank a healthy balance sheet when you start your business, you might find that the manager is amenable to securing any lending to you by means of a bond and floating charge over the assets of the business alone. If this is the case, you will have to set up as a limited company, either private or public. Having done so, your risk element lies only in that amount of capital which you and your other shareholders have injected initially, plus whatever additional assets the business may have in terms of sales invoices due to be paid, along with plant and equipment over which no-one else has a prior claim.

Of course, this is only possible if the value of your business assets is strong enough to justify the faith of the bank manager making the decision, but it can be done. You may find that it is impossible to avoid giving the bank a personal guarantee, even when setting up as a limited company, but the risk to your home has still effectively been minimized, or at least quantified to the tune of the personal guarantee to the bank. If you were a sole trader the risk would be unlimited, and your home and all other assets open to attack by creditors and banks alike, via the appropriate route, in the event of failure of the business. Consider carefully having ownership transferred to your spouse BEFORE starting your business; and take professional advice.

On the other hand, it would be unlikely for a bank to lend readily to any limited company whose balance sheet was weak, and whose shareholding amounted to the probable minimum of £2, unless additional substantial funds had been made available by the owner/manager in the form of long-term loans.

When applying to a bank for a loan for a limited company, it is quite common to be asked for a statement of directors' means, to determine the net worth and credit-worthiness of the individuals who run the company, and possibly to form the basis for any formalized letter of guarantee which might be requested. It could be construed by directors as an intrusion of privacy, especially if they are putting in a substantial investment in the first place. Members of an experienced management team are not umbilically linked to the business like some smaller owner-managed companies.

5. Financial Controls

Banks and investors like to see that there will be a firm grip on the finances of the company by an experienced individual. It helps if this person is an employee and better still an accountant, but this does not mean that you must employ someone specifically to do this on a full-time basis.

Bearing in mind your own resources in terms of time and finance available, it may be that you, in fact, are the only person available, or competent enough, to carry this out. In any event, by working closely with your accountant you can devise an appropriate system for keeping finances under control. This then allows you to provide yourself with management accounts and information about how the company is performing at any time. Not only will this provide an accurate up-to-date picture for you, it will enable lenders or investors to have an extra degree of confidence in your ability to manage their loan or investment.

6. Financial Partners

It is usual for a business to seek finances from more than one source, and it can prove very useful indeed in persuading others to get involved if you can demonstrate the willing participation of a respected and possibly high-profile backer.

You will come across the expression 'gearing' as you toil to raise the required finance for your business. This represents the amount of debt (borrowed money) within a business's finances in relation to the amount of equity (investment). (In Part Two, Chapter Two: *What Sources are Available?* we explained the principles behind equity finance and debt finance). These figures do not take into consideration items like trade credit, only institutional or other lending. Lenders do not really like to lend a business any more than the amount of investment by the shareholders (i.e. 50% gearing), but it is common to find higher gearing (around 75%) where premises or property form the basis for borrowings.

If you are able to persuade your local bank to offer to lend you money for a specific purpose such as working capital, subject to other specialist sources, such as leasing companies, providing assistance with the acquisition of equipment or machinery, you can use this as a lever to get the other parties involved. It doesn't have to be your bank which gets the ball rolling – it might actually be easier to secure finance for vehicles or machinery first of all, since such a specialist source will normally take all or most of the loan risk against the projected value of the vehicles or equipment. Successful negotiation of the first part of the financial package will give you the inner confidence necessary to try and persuade others to get involved, and provide them with visible proof of someone else's belief in your idea.

The hardest part in putting together a financial package is to somehow or other fill the 'equity gap' which may exist in your funding package, if you are to get the gearing to an acceptable level for the bank. Having said that, you will find that it is usually easier to place the last piece in this jigsaw once you have established agreements in principle with the lenders concerned. People generally feel more comfortable with business plans and financial projections once the amounts involved have been quantified, and the sources of financial partners identified.

It is not unknown for business plans to be presented to different sources, showing each one that the other specialist lenders have been lined up in principle, but that the last crucial conclusion of the package depends on them playing their vital role as lender of last resort. People like to think of themselves as being the white knight who saves the day, and can sometimes rise to the occasion magnificently. Once all parties agree to take part providing that everyone else does, there is light at the end of the tunnel.

7. Customers

Your business can only survive if you have customers, and you will have indicated your proposed customer base and how you will attract customers in the Marketing section of the Story. But have you thought about how your customers can actually finance your business for you? The concept is extremely simple. Instead of falling into the trap of allowing your customers to pay you when they feel like it, you set up your business in such a way that they actually pay you either:

Partly in advance   (deposit with order)
Wholly in advance   (payment with order)
Wholly on delivery   (payment on delivery/completion)

Any combination of the above would give you a head start in the financial stakes, and possibly just as importantly, minimize your exposure to cancelled orders. Clients are less inclined to cancel orders where they stand to lose all or a proportion of their money. At least where orders are cancelled and you hold a deposit, you can use it to offset any costs incurred, or generously credit it against their next order to encourage customer loyalty.

If you find that your proposed business is in an industry or service which operates on a mainly cash basis, then you obviously don't need to go through this exercise.

In addition to this method of getting a degree of self-financing from your business, the quality of your customers will tell potential lenders a lot about the quality of your service and your attitude to business. If your sales ledger is going to form part of the security for lenders, they will be comforted to know that you are dealing with companies which have good credit ratings, have been established for some time and do not appear to be in danger of imminent collapse. Many large companies have an appalling track record of late payments to suppliers, preferring instead to invest their vast reserves of cash in short-term or overnight money markets. Indeed, some large companies have come to rely on the money they can earn in this way to bolster their otherwise ailing profits.

The quality of the customer is of paramount importance if, for example, you wish to use the factoring option, since the factoring company will only fund those invoices which it believes to be collectable. The poorer the quality of your customer, the less likely it is that a factoring company will want to accept your invoices to them. This does not mean, however, that factors will only deal with you if you have blue-chip clients, but your customers must have reasonable credit ratings and payment track records.

8. Suppliers

In the same way that your customers are a reflection of your business, so too are your suppliers. Again, you don't have to restrict yourself to big companies for the sake of it, but you do have to illustrate that you have sourced materials etc. from more than one supplier of good standing and reputation to ensure continuity of supply of important goods of an appropriate quality.

Your customers will quickly find alternative sources for the goods or services which you supply, if the goods and services fall below an acceptable quality for them. You cannot afford to allow a poor supplier to destroy your business, so make sure that you manage them properly in a way that suits your business.

Demonstrating to potential lenders and investors that you have a specific supply policy to take into account potential problems in this sensitive area helps to build confidence in you, your team and the business.

You might find that your suppliers realize that they have a vested interest in ensuring your success, and may be willing to negotiate favourable payment terms with you to allow you to get the business started. If you can combine, say, 90 days credit from suppliers with payment in advance by your customers, you have the makings of a winning formula on your hands.

In some instances, this relationship could be developed even further by negotiating a loan from your suppliers or offering them a stake in your business. You might wish to illustrate to them how this could assist your business growth and therefore increased turnover with them, which in itself could more than repay any loan or investment they might make.

You will occasionally find that suppliers who have a detailed understanding of their products and markets can step in and effectively take the place of a bank where the bank is 'running scared' from a particular sector because of a perceived lack of security or confidence in the future of the industry. Once again, scaffolding can be used as an example. Banks don't like the fact that it can be dismantled and is therefore difficult to identify in the event of repossession being necessary. Scaffolding manufacturers or suppliers, particularly when sales are slow, might be persuaded to fund your acquisition of materials. To provide the supplier with a degree of security, it could be done as a hire-purchase type of agreement which allows the supplier to retain title (ownership) of the goods until the agreed amount has bccn paid in full.

9. Security (collateral) within and outwith the business

We have previously mentioned how the unencumbered assets in a limited company can form the basis for security for bank lending, usually in the form of an overdraft. However, an overdraft is not necessarily the right means of financing all aspects of business requirements. There are more and more specialist lenders appearing who offer to provide finance for specific types of capital purchases, e.g.:

- Motor cars
- Commercial vehicles
- Construction plant
- Earth moving equipment
- Printing equipment

In such cases, the loan or financial package is made available to the customer, using the asset's current and projected values as the basis for security or the risk. In many cases they will be cheaper than the equivalent bank loan (if it were available). In addition, the bank will consider that its exposure has been reduced by spreading the finance requirements among several sources.

Should the value of the asset or the strength of your balance sheet be insufficient, you may be asked to provide additional collateral as security, most likely the family home (though see Part Two, Chapter Two, *What Can I Offer as Security?* for additional information). If you live in rented accommodation, then this obviously does not apply at all, as there is no value in your occupancy for any lender.

If you own your home outright, with no mortgage or other loans secured against it, you can use this as security for any business loan which requires it.

If you are buying your home with a mortgage or have an existing loan secured against it, you can use the balance of the value which you effectively own as the collateral for security.

But what security can you actually offer?

If you have a house valued at, say £70,000 and you own it outright, then the bank will look upon 80% of your equity as reasonable security for the loan you are requesting. This means that you can probably borrow up to 80% of £70,000 i.e. £56,000.

If, on the other hand, you have the same house but with a mortgage of £50,000, you can only offer the bank the difference between what you already owe and the current value, i.e.:

	£	
	70,000	value
less	50,000	existing loan
	20,000	equity

But because the bank will only top up your borrowing to a total of 80% of value, i.e. £56,000, you will only be able to borrow another £6,000 from the bank even though you think you've £20,000 equity, i.e.

£	
56,000	maximum lending
50,000	existing loan
6,000	additional borrowing power

This is very important when trying to work out your total financial package and borrowing power. It is even more important to remember that if you cannot keep up your mortgage payments because of a fall in income, you run the risk of repossession, but in addition to this the commercial loan which you may have secured poses similar risks. The security is there for a reason, i.e. to protect the lender. The lender will not hesitate to take steps to have your home repossessed if this is the only way clear to getting the money back. If your borrowing requirements are small, you may be putting your home at disproportionate risk by using it as security. Try to find an alternative, like stocks and shares, life assurance policies, etc. Discuss this carefully with your advisers and the lender beforehand.

The foregoing analysis of the criteria lenders use to evaluate potential clients may seem somewhat heavygoing, but it is well worthwhile giving considerable thought to those areas which are relevant to your own plans and personal circumstances.

You can negotiate a successful package which will set you off on the right track – and it will be easier to achieve if you take the time now to explore every possible avenue and consider every likely eventuality.

> Remember that you will have to pay interest at commercial rates, which are likely to be more expensive than residential mortgage rates, and this might typically be 3 or 4% above the current base rate, which is the reference point most banks will use for setting the cost of money. So, if base rate is, say, 7 % and you are being charged 3% above base, you will be paying a rate of 10% per annum for the money you borrow.

2. Creating your cash flow forecast

Fortunately, there are many sources of help for you in this particular area, not least of which is the fact that your existing bank has probably produced a Starter Pack for would-be entrepreneurs, and this will usually include a pre-printed grid for you to experiment with your projections.

The cash flow forecast can be a salutary lesson in how little things can quickly add up, especially in expenses for your new business. You might find that at the end of the paper exercise you feel not only mentally but physically drained. This is because, when you finally look at the bottom line which will represent the difference between actual income and expenditure, you will probably break out in a cold sweat, quickly followed by a hot flush. You will find that you need to loosen your collar or take off a pullover due to a sudden sharp increase in room temperature, and will start to mutter to yourself such well-used expressions as:

'That can't be right!'
or
'There must be a mistake somewhere!'
or
'I must have added something in twice!'

Rest assured that this is extremely common, and serves to bring sharply into focus three things:

- You'll need to do more of the work yourself without additional pay;
- You must arrange to be paid for your products or services as quickly as is practicable;
- You might not be able to pay your own suppliers as quickly as you had hoped.

The Cash Flow Forecast: getting started
The number of items which you need to list as a source of income or point of expenditure will depend upon the business you intend to set up. The grid provided by your bank (or another source) will contain suggested headings to give you some ideas, but be sure to add your own specific items, or

modify categories to suit your business. (See the sample at the end of this chapter.)

> Since this is your first draft, add in as many items as you can think of initially to let you see what you've allowed for. It is easier for you to spot the absence of something if you've done a detailed breakdown.

Later, once you're satisfied that you've taken account of almost everything, you can group them together under general headings (particularly of cost) to avoid making your final forecast over-fussy for the reader. An important point is to remember to have a general cost item entitled 'Other' or 'Contingency' so that you can make last-minute adjustments without major surgery on your forecast.

If you are familiar with spread-sheet programs, then of course you can use a computer to present and adjust your forecast. This does not necessarily mean that you can abandon pen and paper though, since doing it manually in the beginning enables you to transpose the figures onto computer more quickly later. Because you can rarely view the full year's figures on a computer screen at any one time, a printout or manual forecast sheet has the advantage of allowing you to see all the figures in context at one time.

Remember to enter the figures for the money which you expect to receive and pay out IN THE MONTH WHEN THE PAYMENT

WILL BE MADE, not when the sales invoice (i.e. what you send out to your customers (= money coming IN to the business), is raised or the purchase invoice (i.e. the invoice which your suppliers send to you (= money going OUT of the business), is received. If you intend to operate a cash-based business such as a shop, and pay your bills as you receive them, then your cash flow forecast could double as a Trading and Profit and Loss Account. If credit is given or taken in the course of trade, or if you have work in progress to consider, it might be better to ask your banker or accountant to help you to work out the Trading and Profit and Loss Account.

This guide is intended to help you spot possible gaps in your finances, and to get financial support for the project. You will find banks and accountants sympathetic towards helping you with the more complex aspects of accounting methods, and discussing these aspects helps to form a basis for a future working relationship.

1. Expenditure/Costs
Start your forecast by entering those costs which are already pretty certain, e.g. wages, rent, rates, car lease etc. Show these costs occurring at the appropriate interval: rent might be paid three monthly in advance, rates might be monthly in arrears or every six months.

Using your knowledge and experience, make allowances for the cost of stocks, raw materials and any sub-contract fees.

If you have hire purchase or term loans, you should try to show repayments of the capital (the initial sum borrowed) and interest (the cost of the loan) as separate items, since repayment of capital is not a cost as such, even though you have to find the money from your revenues to pay it each month.

Refer to the example given for guidance: show monthly totals for both Income (1) and Expenditure (2). Your nett cash flow (i.e. surplus or deficit) at (3) is found by subtracting (2) from (1).

If we assume that you start your business with a zero balance in your bank account on day one (see *Bank Opening Balance* (4)), any movement in cash flow terms will dictate what your *Bank Closing Balance* will be (5) at the end of the month. If you have a positive figure at (5) at the end of the month, you would appear to have an adequate financial package in place. On the other hand, if you have a negative figure, this indicates the level of additional funding you might require as additional working capital.

If no other source is available to you, the bank is the most likely lender for this, providing that you can satisfy their requirements in terms of security, either personal or from business assets, or perhaps in the form of a guarantee by a third party such as a benefactor, investor, parent etc.

Even if you can't provide the security, you may be able to use your persuasive skills to show the bank manager how his commercially astute support in this area will make all the difference to the project: just don't overdo it! There are from time to time certain specialist loan schemes for small businesses where the government will guarantee to the bank a certain percentage of any possible shortfall for a premium. Banks tend to be loath to use these schemes because of the paperwork and procedures involved, but be persistent in your quest and ask for all possible sources to be considered.

2. Income/Sales

On your cash flow you should show income from all sources such as term loan from the bank (with a corresponding outgoing section for the purchase of the item on the expenditure section), and cash introduced by you as equity or loans, as well as sales generated or fees earned.

You can arrive at your sales figures in various ways, one of which is based on forecasting the number of units you expect to sell, based on your knowledge, experience and understanding of the market in which you intend to operate. You might wish to back this up with copies of orders or letters of intent from potential clients (be careful that securing orders in advance does not preclude you from any loan or grant scheme).

Another way is to work out how much income you're going to need just to stay in business, and then break this down further into categories of product or service and the number of sales, contracts or individual jobs achievable within each category in order to come up with the necessary income.

Whichever of the above methods you use, you will have already carried out an elementary *break-even analysis* (see below). Your bank manager will not expect you to make huge profits in Year One, so unless you can justify your enthusiastic forecast, use your break-even analysis as the basis for your sales forecast. This will generally satisfy most bank managers, providing that you can also illustrate that there will be an upward trend in income and profitability towards the end of the year which will be sustained in Year Two and subsequent years. You might consider it almost pointless to try to forecast sales etc. for two or three years ahead, but it will probably be necessary to do so. However, you can use this to your advantage, showing that any lack of initial profitability in the setting-up stages will soon be outstripped by healthy profits in subsequent years, due to prudent foundation-building and gradual and controlled expansion. Since your objective is to secure initial funding, and there is relatively little in this world which is certain in the future, a little latitude and optimism is normally allowed (and possibly expected) beyond the first year's forecast, especially if the idea seems to have been proven elsewhere.

Break-even analysis
Do not panic if this expression doesn't seem to belong to any language you recognize. It can be a relatively simple calculation which can be done once you have had an attempt at working out your future costs and income. Your task is to work out what level of sales/income you will need to meet all your expenses (including your own wages/salary), and determine whether or not this is realistic for your business as

you envisage it. If you fall short of break-even in Year One, it is not necessarily the end of the dream, since losses are common in new businesses in the early years. However, there has to be a healthy outlook for the business overall if it is to win, and be worthy of, loans or investment by others, as well as the investment of your own precious time and hard-earned cash.

Example:	Total Costs incurred Year One	£ 29,000
	Income:	
	Consultancy reviews 20 @ £900	18,000
	Shop Design 10@ £1,000	10,000
	Sales Stands 15@ £100	1,500
	Total Sales	29,500
	Surplus	500

Working backward from the cost figures, we can see that there will be a surplus of income over expenditure of £500. Not a fortune, of course, but not a bad result from the first year's activity, since the wages of the proprietor have already been taken into account in the costs. The following year will hopefully show a more consistent earning pattern after the business becomes more established, and should finish the year with a higher level of profitability.

'Understate and Overprove' is a maxim worth remembering. If you are over-ambitious with your sales and profit forecasts and fail to come close to them, the investors or banks lending to you will be most distressed and fear for the future. If, however, you have forecast just enough to justify their support and finish the year at 120% of your target, you will become 'flavour of the month' and will find it easier to get support for future projects.

4. The Closing Summary

This last section should describe how you see your business developing over the initial three years from Start-up, what you hope to have achieved at the end of that time, and how you see the future. Make your ambitions clear: your advisers and lenders need to understand your intentions and how you see these developing. Keep it brief but to the point. You have outlined your aims in the Executive Summary and shown how you hope to achieve these in the Story and the Financial Data. Now is the time to say how you see your project developing. Your motivations and ambitions are important here – small-scale or large-scale – just tell the truth!

5. Appendices

These should include, for example, all the facts, figures and tables you have compiled from your research to support the various sections of the Business Plan; curricula vitae for any directors involved; details of property, vehicles and any other purchases necessary; sample layouts of advertising material and so on.

One final point: if you need to borrow money to start your business, your Business Plan is CRUCIAL. Take time to compile it thoroughly and

make sure you understand it completely
take advice from experts before you submit it
have it professionally typed and properly laid out.

CASE HISTORY
Maureen, co-owner of card and gift shop.

When we took over the business it had been allowed to run downhill so we had a lot of building-up to do. There were unforeseen expenses too, and we only discovered these once we'd moved in. For example we'd allocated money for redecoration but then realized that the carpeting needed to be replaced – that was a huge expense. And although we managed to find a cheaper insurance, the new insurers insisted we replace the Calor gas heating, so again we had an unforeseen additional cost. In fact I'd advise anyone to work out how much they THINK they need and then double it!

We also had to learn about our customers and what kind of products they wanted. The advantage we have, as a private shop compared with the larger chains, is that we can choose what stock we carry; we can take a small, exclusive range of cards, for example, possibly from a local artist, as well as stock from the usual manufacturers. The customers here come from a wide variety of backgrounds so I have to try and please them all! You can learn tricks of the trade as you go on – I try and place plastic-wrapped cards on the lower shelves, for instance, to avoid too much damage from small, sticky fingers! Shoplifting too can be a problem, you need the proverbial eyes in the back of your head. And you have to have a thick skin – people can be very rude.

We've been here a couple of years or so and are only now beginning to show a reasonable profit – you have to take this into account when you start – you still need money to live! I've been working seven days a week, doing the books on a Sunday as we're open six days a week, but I now employ someone to help out to give myself a break. And as if all the paperwork, accounts and ordering wasn't enough, we small shopkeepers are expected to act as unpaid assistants to government departments – collecting National Insurance and PAYE, and taking part in compulsory Customs & Excise surveys into retailing. There's no choice – it's all statutory. But in spite of the gripes, it's all worth it, though; I enjoy the challenge and I enjoy working in the shop; I'm glad we decided to go for it.

Phone	150	150	150	150	150	150	900
Line Rent	150	150	150	150	150	150	900
Stationery	150	150	150	150	150	150	900
Motor Ins.	80	80	80	80	80	80	480
Marketing	4,000	3,200	2,400	1,600	1,200	1,200	13,600
PR	2,000	1,600	1,200	800	600	600	6,800
Audit							
/accs	1,000	800	600	400	300	300	3,400
Legal	1,000	800	600	400	300	300	3,400
Corp. Tax							
Leasing	1,500	500	500	500	500	500	4,000
VAT							
Instal	1,000	1,000					2,000
Train	1,000	1,000	1,000	1,000	1,000		5,000
Totals (2)	15,540	14,320	13,100	11,500	10,700	9,700	74,860
Surplus (3)	46,460	-10,320	-9,100	-5,500	-4,700	-1,700	15,140
Bank open (4)	0	46,460	36,140	27,040	21,540	16,840	
Bank close (5)	46,460	36,140	27,040	21,540	16,840	15,140	

Month:	1	2	3	4	5	6	Total (6 months)
Income							
Sales	2,000	4,000	4,000	6,000	6,000	8,000	30,000
Cash	5,000						5,000
Bank	10,000						10,000
Loan	30,000						30,000
Grant	15,000						15,000
Totals (1)	62,000	4,000	4,000	6,000	6,000	8,000	90,000
Expend							
Wages	2,400	3,600	4,800	4,800	4,800	4,800	25,200
NI	240	360	480	480	480	480	2,520
Material	120	180	240	240	240	240	1,260
Postages	120	120	120	120	120	120	720
Rent	300	300	300	300	300	300	1,800
Rates	150	150	150	150	150	150	900
Prop. Maint.	15	15	15	15	15	15	90
Power	15	15	15	15	15	15	90
Motor	150	150	150	150	150	150	900

							Total
Phone	150	150	150	150	150	150	1,800
Line Rent	150	150	150	150	150	150	1,800
Stationery	150	150	150	150	150	150	1,800
Motor Ins.	80	80	80	80	80	80	960
Marketing	1,200	1,200	1,200	1,200	1,200	1,200	20,800
PR	600	600	600	600	600	600	10,400
Audit /accs	300	300	300	300	300	300	5,200
Legal	400	400	400	400	400	400	5,800
Corp. Tax							
Leasing	500	500	500	500	500	500	7,000
VAT							
Instal							2,000
Train							5,000
Totals (2)	9,800	9,800	9,800	9,800	9,800	9,800	133,660
Surplus(3)	200	200	2,200	2,200	2,200	2,200	24,340
Bank open (4)	15,140	15,340	15,540	17,740	19,940	22,140	
Bank close (5)	15,340	15,540	17,740	19,940	22,140	24,340	

Month:	7	8	9	10	11	12	Total (Year)
Income							
Sales	10,000	10,000	12,000	12,000	12,000	12,000	98,000
Cash							5,000
Bank							10,000
Loan							30,000
Grant							15,000
Totals (1)	10,000	10,000	12,000	12,000	12,000	12,000	158,000
Expend							
Wages	4,800	4,800	4,800	4,800	4,800	4,800	54,000
NI	480	480	480	480	480	480	5,400
Material	240	240	240	240	240	240	2,700
Postages	120	120	120	120	120	120	1,440
Rent	300	300	300	300	300	300	3,600
Rates	150	150	150	150	150	150	1,800
Prop. Maint.	15	15	15	15	15	15	180
Power	15	15	15	15	15	15	180
Motor	150	150	150	150	150	150	1,800

PART THREE

GETTING
STARTED

1. MARKETING AND SELLING

Estate Agents have got a lot to answer for in confusing the use of the terms 'selling' and 'marketing'. If you wish to sell your home, and you discuss the services offered by estate agents, you will find that they quickly and miraculously substitute the word 'marketing' where you would normally use the word 'selling'. This is presumably to inflate your ego, as well as the perceived value of their service and justify their charges, on the basis that they are engaged in the art of marketing, not selling, your home. After all, marketing sounds terribly professional, doesn't it? This is not to decry the services of a good estate agent, of course, but let us try to distinguish between the two activities.

Marketing

The study of trends, needs and wants of a pool of potential clients in order to design, modify or otherwise provide products or services which can be sold at a profit to fulfil these requirements.

Selling

The identification of the needs and wants of potential clients, combined with the illustration to the clients of how the purchase of a given product or service can fulfil those requirements. The successful sale provides a benefit to the buyers and a profit to the sellers, satisfying both parties.

The Principles of Marketing

In advising on the preparation of both the Outline Business Plan and the formal Business Plan, we suggested that you undertake some preliminary market research and analysis to support your conviction that there is a demand for your product or service. Deciding the *target market*, the *unique selling point* and *company image* was part of this exercise. In this section we look in greater detail at the principles of marketing and suggest various marketing methods you could consider using for your product or service. The type of marketing operation you set up will, naturally, depend on the type of business and the probable competition. If you are starting a local painting/decorating business, for example, a leaflet campaign around local houses might be sufficient; but if you intend setting up a specialist design consultancy, you might need to advertise in appropriate magazines, as well as the local, and possibly national, press.

Whatever your business, it is worthwhile spending some time considering the basic principles of marketing which, today, has become a highly-sophisticated operation.

In marketing circles, the principles of marketing are referred to as *The Four 'P's*. These are:

1. Product: the goods or service that are created and offered for sale.
2. Price: that indicator of value or quality which is requested in payment.

3. Promotion: the methods used to expose/present products to potential buyers.
4. Place: the physical location of your enterprise and/or products.

The purpose of your market research activity is to allow you to blend together the right combination of factors within the Four P's in order to achieve maximum success. The type of business which you will create will determine the details of each category.

1. Product

Are you setting off with a pre-determined product, which requires you to quantify the existing market? Or are you researching the market with an open mind in order to identify problems which can be resolved by products which you will create to provide solutions? If you are not tied to a single product or manufacturer you are in a far stronger position to take advantages of trends and fashions within your chosen marketplace, and can create your own portfolio or range of products or services to meet current demand. This applies to business-to-business sales situations as much as to retailers.

2. Price

If you try to be the cheapest supplier, you might find that your product or service is perceived to be of low quality.

Competing on price alone is a dangerous practice, and can be difficult to sustain in the long term. Forget about trying to base your pricing on formulas such as 'cost plus 20%.' Find out what customers are currently paying for any similar products, and whether or not they are prepared to pay even more for your superior product. People generally use price as an indicator of quality, so the higher the price of something, the better it is thought to be. There is nothing to prevent you from setting a premium price for your product, which can then be discounted for purchases in bulk, regular customers, pre-payment, cash on delivery or other suitable offer which does not reduce the perceived value of your product. One aspect of this is that you might be horrified at what at first appear to be enormous profit margins being made. Once you get started, however, you will become aware that there is good reason for margins being at the level they are: the market share which you or any other competitor can achieve is likely to be much less than originally imagined; and your overheads will quickly eat into what might, at first, appear to be a handsome profit!

On the other hand, you might want to price your products low in order to achieve higher volumes of sales. Great care must be taken to make sure that you achieve the high volumes of sales necessary, and that you are able to cover all your costs. Be sure to allow for bad debts and late payers, which of course cost you money in lost profits and extra bank charges.

Once you know the volume of sales likely to be sustainable, you can work out whether your pricing policy is one that is right for your business, and modify it as necessary. Whichever method you use to set your prices, it is obvious that you need to earn sufficient profit to cover your overheads and the direct expenses incurred in running your business.

Earlier we spoke about needs and wants. Each of these provides a buyer with some motivation to buy, but what is the difference? If you're considering redecorating the kitchen because you don't like the colour any more, that is a WANT. But if you've had a burst pipe in the bathroom and your kitchen decor has been ruined, then you NEED to have it redecorated! Put yourself in each position. How important do you think price will be in each case?

3. Promotion
This covers all aspects of getting your business known, contacting potential clients, and presenting them with your products.

Advertising
Was it Henry Ford who once said 'Half the money I spend on advertising is a waste – the trouble is, I don't know which half!'?

It is very easy indeed to spend money on advertising which has absolutely no guarantee of a return, but here the fledgling business has the advantage of being able to identify clearly those publications whose readership most closely matches their target market before committing valuable cash resources.

There are bound to be local advertising agencies which can advise you on the most appropriate medium for your products, and whose costs are often covered by the commissions paid to them by the newspaper or publication used. Additional costs such as design of adverts or corporate image can sometimes be eligible for a substantial contri-bution from the local council planning department or government-backed enterprise agency. Ask the agents for information about this, but if they aren't aware of any grants, check for yourself directly with the possible sources.

Sales and Promotional Literature
Product leaflets, brochures, business cards and headed paper all come under this category. If you intend to be in direct contact with clients or potential clients, a well-designed business card with your corporate logo and descriptive but not overcrowded text can be a great conver-sation opener and way of generating interest in you and your firm. Similarly, a letterhead which carries the corporate message or style will reinforce your company's image in the eyes of the client, and outline the range of valuable services

which you offer. The use of colour can be eye-catching but also garish, cheapening your image. Use it with caution, or try using a half-tone of the main colour used for your text (best black or dark blue) to add interest without overdoing it. (See this section, Part Two, *Organizing Your Business*, for further help on company stationery).

A colour brochure might be beyond your budget in the early stages of your business, but you will often find that your suppliers will be happy to provide you with promotional material which they have had produced. You can incorporate this into a presentation folder or pack without having to spend a small fortune in printing and design costs. A relatively inexpensive way to do this is to have your local printer produce a cost-effective number (possibly minimum 250 -500) of plain white A4 card folders with your company details and logo overprinted on the front. Inside you can insert the appropriate loose-leaf product information such as that mentioned above. If you are producing your own leaflet or other style, avoid the temptation to try to have too much text on the page. Use the power of images to get your message across where possible.

Direct Mail
This is a useful way of quickly raising the awareness profile of your business, but tends not to appear terribly successful in prompting a response from potential clients. Response rates will vary from 1% for mail that is addressed to 'The

Managing Director' to possibly 4 or 5% for mail properly addressed to 'John Smith, Managing Director'. However, this is not a guarantee of success, since it will also depend on you having carefully targeted your readership and prepared a letter and sales literature which is in some way relevant to the recipient. Of course, a response is not a sale, and it is possible that you will have to deal with success rates of as little as 1 to 10% from those responding. You can imagine that if you have to mailshot 1,000 clients and talk to as many as 100 respondents before you achieve only one sale, your mailshot and pre-sales wages budget might have to be substantial. If you have the money, there are specialist fulfilment houses who offer to handle the total package of targeting your market, buying-in data and mailing lists, and designing, mailing and following-up your direct mail campaign for you. You will probably think that their charges are high, but once you've tried to do it yourself you'll appreciate the time-saving nature of their services. Again, there's nothing to stop you talking to the experts to see how you might work together to get maximum value from your budget. You can boost the effectiveness of your mailshot considerably by using a telephone call to follow-up the letter sent, but again you risk incurring substantial costs and investment of your time if doing so on any scale.

Mailing lists can be purchased (more usually 'rented' for once-only use) from a variety of sources. Suppliers of such data must be licensed under the Data Protection Act, and you will find that contacting a body such as the British Direct

Mail Association can save you time and effort in selecting the appropriate supplier. These lists can be supplied in the form of sticky labels for putting onto your envelopes, along with, possibly, a follow-up call sheet with more details of how to contact the firm by telephone, their turnover level, activity etc. as specified by you. Alternatively, and more popular now, is to have the list provided on a computer disk, which can be used to reproduce the information using your computer; the name of the contact and all the target company's details can be integrated into a personalized letter using a standard text relevant to the type of client. This will allow you to make your letters look more tailored to individual clients, and help to get your message across more effectively.

Telemarketing or Telesales

Again, a slight overlap in the use of 'marketing' and 'sales' is often found in this area. There are some businesses where the telesales department is there to respond to enquiries generated through other forms of promotion. The combination of instant response from television, radio and newspaper advertising with specialist direct sales operations such as insurance companies and airlines has seen an explosive growth in the number of such Call Centres throughout the country. It is proving to be an extremely efficient and profitable way of generating enquiries and converting them to sales, but tends to be the reserve of companies operating on a considerable scale. There might be as many as a hundred or more staff manning the phones at some Call Centres.

If you have the kind of business where repeat orders are generated from an established client-bank, then you might be able to use the telephone to your advantage by having office-based staff calling your clients to check on their current requirements for stock at the appropriate time. This has the advantage of freeing yourself or your sales staff from what could be fairly routine but 'comfortable' selling, and allows the time saved 'in the field' to be spent in the pursuit of new clients.

The telephone is the most powerful tool available to any sales organization, and can be used to good effect to open many doors which are closed to the salesperson who dares to attempt to call in person. It would be a mistake to assume that in all telesales situations the phone is used to make a sales pitch and close a deal over the phone. It simply won't work for most products. The telephone contact should be used for:

- Initial contact and information gathering;
- Getting through to the decision makers;
- Qualifying their requirements to confirm that you have a benefit to offer;
- Making the appointment for a face-to-face sales meeting.

Face-to-Face Selling

Many people shy away initially from the idea of selling, but when you really believe in what you're offering the customers, there's no more rewarding job. Contrary to popular belief, good sales people are made, not born, but it helps if you are born with some of the characteristics of a good salesperson, e.g.

- Drive;
- Enthusiasm;
- Tenacity;
- Self-confidence;
- Resilience.

Funnily enough, these are also some of the characteristics needed by successful entrepreneurs, so don't worry if you've never had direct sales experience before. The very fact that you've got to this stage means that you must have some, if not all, of these, and possibly more. With some additional training and an awareness of how to structure a successful sale, your confidence will grow and your performance improve rapidly. Sometimes a person is said to be a 'born salesman/saleswoman' and indeed some very successful sales people enter this field late in life and with no prior formal training in sales. Their natural enthusiasm and belief in the product is what makes them successful, combined with an understanding of what their clients need or want. When you start in business for yourself, you take on some of the characteristics of the born salesman or woman without realising it, and very soon you will be adding practical professional selling experience to your natural charms and abilities. Invest in sales training for yourself and your staff. It will more than repay itself.

This extremely important component of your marketing mix is being given more and more recognition of the status it deserves. On average, one successful salesperson keeps another six people in employment by the various support services required such as administration, technical maintenance, component manufacture etc. In Chapter Two of this section, *Successful Selling for Beginners*, we offer some practical advice on how to present your new business to its best advantage to potential customers and how to conclude those vital sales!

Networking

This is the buzz-word used to describe how people use interaction with other business people to widen their circle of contacts and open up new areas of possible business opportunities. If you are a member of a sports or social club you already have the basis of a personal network. Your friends and family may not in themselves be able to become clients, but they can provide you with another dimension to your network by thinking about their own friends and contacts who could be in the market for your products. A particularly useful source of business contacts is your local or regional Chamber of Commerce. Interestingly, there is no legislation in the UK which stipulates that you have to belong to a Chamber, but there is in France and Germany, for example, and this makes their network of Chambers of Commerce even more important and influential than in the UK. Nonetheless, the UK Chambers of Commerce provide you with a positive opportunity to make contact with other businesses. It's up to you to make the most of it, and it's also a very inexpensive way of keeping up to date with legislation and other developments likely to affect your business.

Other sources for networking are national and local business clubs, trade and professional associations, gentlemen's clubs, and more ladies' business clubs which seem to be springing up to cater for the hitherto largely independent (through necessity) businesswoman.

Public Relations

Get yourself talked about! This might be easier than you think. Local newspapers are usually on the look-out for good news about new jobs in the area. If you can combine that with an interesting angle such as the world's first domestic widget polishing machine being produced locally, together with discussions with a major foreign potential customer with regard to selling the overseas distribution licences, you'll have the press, radio and TV eating out of the palm of your hand. Sponsor the local girl guides or scout football team and you'll be remembered by the grateful parents. Dream up the XYZ prize for outstanding performance in woodwork for local schools and get your picture in the paper awarding the first of many prizes.

You can use a professional firm to do this for you as a means of complementing your advertising, or you might find that you or one of your team get a kick out of fostering these relationships yourselves. Like most other tasks, it can become quite time-consuming and take your eye off the main business objective of making money. And because it can be great fun to do all this, be careful not to get too involved as a means of avoiding your real work!

4. Place

There are three important things to remember about having a successful business, especially a retail outlet, hotel, pub or anything dependent on passing trade. These are:

Location, Location and Location!

Have you got the idea? This is a well-known expression used frequently by experienced retailers and property professionals. Bear it in mind in any business.

How will you be selling your products or services? If you need to have a high street or other main road location, get the best you can afford. Remember that the cost of renting quality premises will soon appear to be a bargain when you compare it with the wages bill at the end of the year. It is important for any business to be able to access its market easily, but for some this can mean using efficient postal services (mail order) and/or road, rail and air transport links (delivery and distribution services). Consider also the need for access to high quality telephone links (Call Centre operation; see above, telemarketing or telesales). If you need specialist staff to work for you, accessibility to your offices or work place will be of vital importance; there's no point in offering the best product or service in the world if you can't recruit the staff necessary to see it through.

2. SUCCESSFUL SELLING FOR BEGINNERS

To the uninitiated, the idea of being a salesperson can be quite daunting because of the fear of the unknown and the fear of rejection. There is also the negative impression of selling which is largely the product of exposure to over-eager and newly recruited time-share touts or even insurance salesmen – 'all that forcing people to buy things they don't really want at prices they can't really afford'. However, in reality the job of the salesperson is quite simple: to ensure that there are always two winners when a sale is concluded – a satisfied buyer and a contented seller. The success of the salesman or saleswoman in satisfying clients will also open other doors for him or her: the clients will normally be delighted to recommend you and introduce you to their friends, or even the competition, if they believe that you can help them too. The success of a salesperson is directly in proportion to two main points:

• Belief in the product

  and

• Enthusiasm

A well-used expression in sales is
'There is only one thing more infectious than enthusiasm, and that is THE LACK OF IT!'

The job of selling can be very rewarding, both financially and psychologically – there is nothing like the heady feeling of euphoria felt when the first-ever sale has been made! And once you've encountered success, this lifts the spirit even further, spurring you on to further confident activity and sales. You will, however, like everyone else who's ever been in sales, encounter moments when you wish the earth would open up and swallow you, but you must try to keep your spirits up and avoid showing the world how you really feel. After all, if you go into a pub, for example, and the staff serving you are surly and rude, you are hardly going to feel like staying there for long to tolerate their unpleasant behaviour, are you? They are in the public eye, and their role is to 'sell' the atmosphere in the pub, not just dispense the drinks.

It's all very well being enthusiastic about your products, but of course you really do need to believe that they will provide your potential clients with real benefits – it's not enough to want to sell something just because you know it will earn you a bonus. Product knowledge is indispensable in order to understand how the purchase can and will benefit the customer. If you get to know how the customer's business works, and what the priorities are in serving his or her clientele, then you can ensure that you are selling the correct product to fulfil these requirements. It is the combination of product knowledge and empathy with your customers that allows you to have belief in your products. Remember that you are not simply selling an article or service, you are providing a solution to a problem, whether that problem is to find a hard-wearing pair of trousers which look smart and businesslike for wearing to work, or organizing programmed maintenance for machinery to avoid wasted production time.

So how do you get started in selling? It will depend on:

- the kind of products or services you are selling;

- the clientele you are servicing;

- the place where you do it.

1. Shops and other retail establishments

In this situation, the client is making an effort in coming to you, and it is important to welcome and acknowledge the client when they enter your premises. All that is required at this stage is a simple 'Good morning'. The use of 'sir' or 'madam' is largely a matter of shop policy or personal choice, but there is nothing worse than walking into a shop and being completely ignored by staff. Most people would take the opportunity to walk straight back out of the door again - wouldn't you? (Anyone recently returned to the UK from the USA will notice a marked difference in standards of service.) Once the client has entered the shop or section that you are working in, it is important to make further contact and make it easy for them to let you know why they are there. An opening question which invites a conversational response, such as 'Are you looking for something for yourself or is it for someone else?' will help your customer open up and provide you with the further information which your will need to assist them. Further prompting like 'What sort of an occasion will it be for?' or 'Do you have any particular styles that you wish to avoid?' will get things going between you. You will soon become quite relaxed about how to approach the different types of people that you will encounter, and realize how much 'space' each type will need to allow them to feel comfortable enough to make the right purchase. Another point which is extremely important in retail situations is that the customer, having made up his or her mind to make a purchase, is at their most receptive to other sales ideas. So if someone has gone out to buy a suit, he might well see the logic in getting new shoes, shirts, ties and cufflinks to show it off to best advantage.

Watch what happens to you next time you go into a shop or hotel. Do the staff smile? Do they welcome you or avoid you? The cardinal sin of selling is committed every day by shopkeepers and assistants throughout the country – the conversation stopper of a closed question like 'Can I help you?' What would your answer be? Probably, 'No thanks, I'm just having a look.' Don't fall into the trap of doing what everyone else does, just do it right and be yourself. Remember, a 'closed question' is one which invites a 'yes' or 'no' response; an 'open question' invites further elaboration, such as 'What sort of function will you be attending in this outfit?' Open questions open up the conversation; closed questions close it down.

2. Personal Direct Selling

By this we mean the salesperson endeavouring to sell a product by means of a direct presentation to a potential customer, probably in the customer's business premises. The first step to success in personal direct selling is to do some preliminary research to enable you to target your most likely potential customers. By taking the trouble to do this at the outset, you will save valuable time and energy later.

Prospecting

This is the act of sifting through the data available on what you consider to be potential customers, and the qualification (or filtering) via your own criteria to establish which offers the best potential for you.

There are some businesses (such as selling weighing equipment to independent retail shops like grocers, butchers, etc.) which can only carry on their prospecting and sales activity in one way, and that is by salesmen appearing on the doorstep during business hours with the intention of a brief meeting, introductory discussion, and possibly a fixed appointment to return or sometimes an opportunity to carry out a demonstration there and then. In this case, it is relatively easy to identify your target market, since a quick drive around the area will allow you to spot those shops which appear to fit the bill for your products.

For other businesses, such as selling computer software programs for accountants, it should be possible to buy a directory, yearbook or mailing list which allows you to gather more detailed information about your potential customers before making contact. If your potential market lies in accountancy practices with more than twenty employees, for example, this is the type of information which can often be uncovered by research, with the result that you can whittle down the numbers that you will need to contact, thus saving time and effort.

Qualifying the prospects using telesales

The quickest and often most cost-effective way of further qualifying your prospect is to call them and ask the receptionist a few brief questions to see whether they have the necessary characteristics for your future clients. So, you might need to find out, for example, whether they offer specialist tax advice, or perform payroll services or whatever is relevant to your users, before asking for the more personal information such as 'Is Mr. Smith the senior partner responsible for this area of activity?' followed by 'Is he in?' and then 'Could you put me through to him please?'

The secret in all successful selling is in the preparation done prior to the call. In the case of telephone work, whether to gather basic or more advanced information, this means having a logical pattern to your questioning, and if necessary a script for you to follow. You will soon be able to work without a detailed script, and our advice would be to write down the key words for the topics you intend to cover, simply to prompt you about the next part of your call and ensure that you don't miss anything out. This also has the benefit of allowing you to sound more natural, and to phrase the questions in a way that is more comfortable for you.

The great advantage of using the telephone is that you or your business can make contact with an enormous number of potential clients in a very short space of time. You can gather a vast amount of information which lets you know how likely each prospect is to turn into a client based on their business profile, and the information about the timing of their purchases allows you to plan a calling programme for you or your sales team. The reason that this method of pre-sales qualification is so popular is that the cost of a salesperson's time is so high these days that to be most effective they should not be wasting their valuable time gathering basic information. A salesperson is most effective when sitting down with a client whose needs have been determined by telesales methods, and who is receptive to information on products or services for which he or she has a proven or latent need. Success rates for sales people are often referred to as 'hit rates' or 'strike rates', and to illustrate this we can use the following example:

10,000 'cold' calls by phone might generate 100 'warm' leads to follow up (1 in 100)

100 'warm' leads might generate only 10 sales (1 in 10)

If a salesperson's time in a month normally generates the following activity:

1,000 'cold' calls leading to 10 'warm' leads

10 'warm' leads generating 1 sale

it is not difficult to see the attractiveness in using telesales in boosting the absolute level of sales generated by one salesperson by a factor of 10, providing that the additional cost of carrying out the telesales activity is not more than the additional profit generated.

The sales pitch

Now that you've managed to get in front of the client you have a chance to make your pitch proper. It's easy to get carried away and launch into a torrent of verbal praise for you, your company and its products, but to do so might be wasting the opportunity now facing you. There are four key aspects of selling which will stand you in good stead, and which form the basis for any salesperson's armoury.

KISS

This stands for 'Keep It Simple, Stupid!'

Whatever you do, remember that if you have a detailed knowledge of the technical aspects of your product, it is likely that your customer does not. Unless you know that this is NOT the case because of prior knowledge, avoid describing things in technical detail that your client will pretend to understand before giving you the polite brush-off. After all, when you switch on your hi-fi all you want to know is how to switch it on, use it, and enjoy the benefit of the quality of the sound reproduced. (Well, most of us might want to know the latest buzz-word for the technology, but unless we're engineers, that's about the limit of our desire for knowledge.) If you discover that the most important aspect for your potential client is its non-scratch cover, play that up as much as you can.

AIDA: The structure of a sale
This stands for

> Approach
> Interest
> Desire
> Action

This is useful to you in every sales or pre-sales situation.

Approach
Research and identify your market, select your potential targets and qualify them as much as possible in advance.

Interest

Having established that there is an extremely good chance of your target customer's needs matching the benefits that your products have to offer, and got the client to confirm what his or her needs and wants are, you should be able to move proceedings closer to the conclusion of the sales process by using questions like the following: 'So, Mrs. Smith, if I understand you correctly, you would be interested in looking at our products if we could demonstrate cost saving of 10% per annum on your existing set up?' This leads us neatly to the next stage.

Desire

This is normally encouraged by means of a presentation of how your product can fulfil his or her needs, either physically, if feasible, to show the equipment etc. under discussion, or by showing testimonials from clients or other evidence from existing installations of a similar nature. It may also be necessary to provide the client with a working sample on a trial basis. If so, this should only be done on the understanding (written, if possible) that satisfactory performance will mean the purchase by the client has been concluded.

Action

This means closing the sale and getting your new client officially to confirm the order. Usually you will run through the list of requirements as set out by the client, and get the client to confirm that he or she has been or can be satisfied by your product. This is not the time to shy away from asking for the order by uttering things like 'Fine, I'll wait until we hear from you then.' You must, and your client will expect you to, ask for the order. You can do this in a variety of ways, it's simply a matter of finding out what makes you feel comfortable when doing so. Some people favour the Assumptive Close, which means closing proceedings by producing your order form or book and asking a question like:

'Will delivery to this address be OK?'

Others like to be less direct, and might use the 'Alternative Close' such as:

'Will delivery be to this address or to your stores at London Road?'

Whatever method you use, you will be doing both yourself and your client a favour by being quite confident that this is the logical conclusion to your discussions, which will reassure him or her that the correct decision has been taken. Once you have asked the question, it is extremely important to do only one thing – SHUT UP! Do not be tempted to fill what you might think is an awkward silence if the client does not immediately grasp the pen and sign. If you think that he or she might have doubts, let the client tell you if this is the case. More often than not he or she will simply be rationalizing the positive decision to go ahead, and if you break this train of thought you risk losing the sale altogether.

Remember:

'Who speaks next – loses!'

In fact, if you have done your job properly, the client, who SHOULD be the next to speak, does not lose. Both parties stand to benefit from a successful sale, but this expression is used to help you to understand the importance of keeping quiet once you have asked for the order.

ABC: Always Be Closing

In other words, your conversation should be peppered with expressions which give your customer the maximum number of opportunities to say 'Yes.' This helps to create an extremely powerful atmosphere where it is being confirmed that your discussions will lead logically to a sale. When going through your sales pitch, you should start to use closed questions, the answers to which should be positive, and which confirm the appropriateness of your product in fulfilling the client's requirements, e.g. 'So, Mr. Bloggs, the wide range of colour options means that the equipment will complement your existing colour scheme quite nicely, won't it?' The more often you hear 'Yes', the more confident you should be of a sale when you finally 'close'. If in fact in the course of your presentation it becomes obvious that the client is ready to buy NOW, even though you haven't, in your opinion, completed the pitch, have the presence of mind to read the signals and bring matters to a logical conclusion there and then. Don't feel that you've been cheated of an opportunity to perform – you've succeeded in getting the sale.

USP: Unique Selling Point

Every product has one if you look hard enough. Do you know what yours is? If you don't you'd better find out and use it to your advantage when making a presentation. It may be something as simple as your product being easy to clean, with no dangerous sharp edges or dirt traps, but if your competition is selling products which trap dirt and breed disease, you've got a head start on them. In conjunction with your knowledge of your own products, of course, you'll need to know a good deal about the competition's products too, so that you can work out what your USP really is.

Sell benefits, not features

This means that you have to think about what your product really does for the customer. Being easy to clean is a feature, not a benefit. The benefit is, for example, that it is more hygienic and that there is, therefore, no danger of food poisoning for clients; in addition, easy cleaning means savings in staff time therefore lower wage costs. Generally, time is money in business, so savings in time lead to savings in financial terms too - a matter very close to the heart of almost everyone in business. Whenever you point out a feature of your product, ask yourself from the buyer's perspective, 'So what?' or 'What's in that for me?', this will force you to dig deeper and work out what the real benefit is. Look at the example given in the section *USP – Unique Selling Point* – what is the true benefit?

Dealing with objections

An objection is a request for further information. This simple definition should always be in your mind when talking to clients or making a specific sales pitch.

If you have gone through the qualification process properly before making an attempt actually to sell something, then you have done a significant part of the hard work by making sure that you are talking to someone who has a latent, or actual, need or want which you can satisfy with your product or service.

Nonetheless, it is inevitable that the client will have a natural resistance to being 'sold to'. If you can, make your presentation in such a way that the client is the one who matches the features and benefits of the product with his own needs or wants.

If you are familiar with your products and the needs of the general clientele, then you should be able to pre-empt many potential objections by covering them in your presentation. After all, you are probably the only person who knows all the possible reasons that a client could give for NOT buying whatever you have to sell. Presumably it is the benefits of your product over the competition that led you to want to sell it in the first place – use this as part of your story in the build-up to the sale.

> 'If the salesperson says it's true, it could be a lie. If the client says it's true, it must be true.'

Any salesperson will tell you that the worst possible client to have to make a presentation to is the one who says absolutely nothing. Customers who have an opinion and something to object to are simply screaming out for more detail on how you can solve their problem or satisfy their needs.

When a customer puts up an objection, you can treat it in various ways, such as:

> ignore it
> deal with it
> defer it and deal with it later

Ignore it
If it seems to be a flippant tactic by the customer simply to derail you from your presentation, you can literally ignore an objection, and carry on without attempting to answer it. If the same objection continues to crop up, however, it may be genuine, and you should attempt to dig a little deeper to establish the true nature of it. The customer might say, for example,

'It doesn't fit my kitchen.'

You may think that you have explained clearly the different size options available, but this point seems to be saying that the client doesn't know that. Don't be tempted to give a frosty reply that you've already explained that at some length – you obviously haven't done it well enough for this particular customer. Go back to that point courteously, make sure that it's properly explained, check to establish its importance, go for a trial close by saying something along the lines of, 'So, if we can supply one that fits your kitchen perfectly, can we go ahead with the order?' There may be other objections to overcome yet, so don't push the client too much if you can sense that he or she needs more information and explanation.

Try at all times to put an objection into context; for example, 'It's too expensive' might be dealt with by replying:

'Do you mean that you would find it difficult to hand over £10,000 in one go? So would I, but most people find that our specially negotiated loan facility through the ABC Bank allows them to have the item they want by putting half down as a deposit and paying only £150 per month. What sort of a monthly budget do you think would suit you?'

By agreeing with the objection, you take the sting out of it, create an empathy with the client's situation and your own situation, and allow him or her to feel comfortable with the fact that most people finance it the way you propose. Finally, you put the ball back in their court by giving them the chance to tell you what sort of monthly budget they could comfortably afford.

Treat every objection with respect, and deal with it in an

interested manner. You are dealing with matters which are important to both parties: your livelihood and the customer's hard-earned cash.

If all else fails, and you can't find the key to getting the customer finally to agree, draw up two columns on one side of a blank page: head one column 'for' and the other 'against'. Ask the customer to help you by writing down those reasons, already discussed, in favour of the sale, such as affordable, efficient, stylish, money-saving, impressive performance and so on. Use as many positive reasons as you can possibly remember. Once you've got a healthy list under the 'for' column, pass the paper and pen to the customer and ask him or her to make up the list 'against'. The customer will have great difficulty in coming up with more than a few (especially if you're not prompting too much) and when you compare the number or reasons 'for' with the number 'against' he or she will have difficulty saying 'No'.

Apart from the fact that the customer is possibly lying to you about affordability, you might find that the old chestnut 'I want to think about it' is used to avoid having to make a decision for or against the purchase. You should not be put off by this, since you have a genuine belief in the relevance of this product for the client. Your answer should be similar to this: 'I agree that it is an important decision that deserves full consideration. Since I am here now, and any queries you may have can be answered fully, let's go through the areas which you're uncertain about. Now, what were they?' If you leave the customer now without the order, you can almost certainly forget about it for good!

Selling is about empathy with the customer, product knowledge, and controlling the structure of the sale.

If you can't get the sale, and you still can't work out what the true objection is, leave with good grace.

3. ORGANIZING YOUR BUSINESS

1. THE OFFICE
Information systems: document creation, storage and retrieval.

What do you need?
Each individual business – hairdresser, management consultancy, advertising agency, driving school, garden care, clock repairer – naturally needs its own special equipment, but all businesses need adequate information systems, that is, basic document creation, storage and retrieval. What you need will, of course, depend on the nature and size of your business, but the following represents general guidelines for the efficient running of the administrative side of a business.

Document creation
Computer Systems
Computers are becoming standard equipment in many businesses now and can be used for so many functions, from graphic design, sales databases and product information to basic word processing (letters, invoices and so on), that it may be worthwhile investing in one. If you have no experience of computers, you could ask friends and colleagues what systems they use and discuss how these might be appropriate for you. Tell salespeople what you want the computer to do for you and ask questions – don't be afraid to admit ignorance. We might well be firmly part of the Age of Technology, but there are probably as many technophobes as technophiles around!

- Analyse your needs – make notes if you prefer – and bear these always in mind when considering which system to buy.

- Don't be bamboozled by 'high tech' sales talk; ask questions and insist on clear explanations.

- If the salesperson shows signs of irritation, then go elsewhere.

- Check out the availability of second-hand machines from reputable shops.

If you are totally unfamiliar with computers it may be worthwhile sending yourself on a short training course, rather than spend hours of frustration trying to teach yourself from a manual.

Paperwork – word processor or typewriter?
Word processor
This is a computer system that can deal with all the basic needs of office administration. Depending upon which program (software) is installed it can be used for keeping accounts, compiling databases (e.g. address lists), writing letters, standard invoicing and much more. If you are anticipating a fair amount of routine paperwork, then a word processing system, with its ability to 'memorize' and 'file' information in the appropriate place, would possibly be the most useful for you. In

addition you will need a printer. Word processing programs have become more and more user-friendly over the years and are not difficult to learn.

Printer

In addition to your word processing package you will need a printer. The quality of the printer you buy (and the price you pay!) will depend on what you need it for. Again, discuss this with friends and colleagues as well as salespeople. There are considerable price differences between, for example, inkjet and laser printers; and the amount of printing you can expect from an inkjet cartridge will vary from the amount you can expect from a laser cartridge. Take into account both capital costs and running costs.

Standards of printing have risen to very high levels in recent years with the growth in the use of word processors and electronic typewriters. Well-printed documents can do much to establish the good image of your business, so buy the best printer you can afford.

Typewriter

If your business does not require the resources of a computer, at least not yet, you will almost certainly need a typewriter for business letters, invoices and so on. Electronic typewriters are now very sophisticated and can include a range of typefaces, correction facilities and even a limited memory – useful if you are typing a number of similar letters with only the name and address changed; some even have facilities for copying material onto computer disks.

Photocopier

Photocopiers are now complex pieces of machinery and can carry out some very sophisticated tasks. Like all complex machines, however, photocopiers need regular maintenance and have a great predilection for breaking down, costing time and money, not to mention frustration, to keep in good order. Unless you will need to do substantial amounts of regular photocopying, it may not be necessary, initially, to buy or rent your own machine. High Street franchises, such as Prontoprint and Dittoprint, can offer photcopying facilities at reasonable rates and have experienced staff who can undertake a wide range of special tasks quickly and efficiently.

Document storage
Filing

One of the essential requirements of a well-run office is the ability to find the information you need quickly and accurately. It is, therefore, worthwhile spending some time at the beginning thinking about what kind of information you need to keep and how best you can store it. The quantity and variety of information will depend very much on the nature and size of your business, but the following categories should cover most kinds of work:

1. Office – staff, advertising, insurance, correspondence, PAYE.

2. Accounting – sales, purchases, invoices, banking, receipts, rent and rates.
3. Legal – contracts, leases.
4. Sales – price lists, sales figures, correspondence, product information.
5. Equipment – office equipment and furniture, company cars, vans and other special company equipment

Use this list as a general guide and choose which categories would be appropriate for your own business. A self-employed gardener who works alone, for example, might need categories 2, 4 and 5, but not 1 or 3; whereas a car hire company would need all five.

> Keep only one diary and address book for personal and professional use – and keep it up-to-date!

Storage
Electronic filing
If you have decided to invest in a computer system with the appropriate software, you can use the computer's memory, supplemented by floppy disks (electronic filing) as your basic filing system. However you MUST make regular back-ups on floppy disks or tape in case your system 'crashes' and you lose all the data stored on the computer's hard disk.

Storage systems
These range from the familiar grey filing cabinets with hanging files to card indexes, box files, concertina files and lever arch

files. Again, the key points here are how many different kinds of documents will you need to store and what will the likely quantity be? If you are buying filing cabinets, remember that these can often be bought very reasonably from dealers in second-hand office furniture.

> Open a file when it is needed and file all paperwork as soon as possible.

Classification of documents

Before you choose a method of filing, consider what kind of information you need to keep. Is it company names and addresses? Customer profiles? Product information? Sales information? Addresses of properties? and so on. In general, the simpler the method of classification, the better. Below are some of the more common methods.

Alphabetical order by name e.g. Smith, Robert & Co
Williams and Williams

Geographical order e.g. South East – Eastbourne
Rochester

Type of business e.g. builders   Jackson & Jackson
Stewart & Son
plumbers   Acme Plumbing Systems
First Class Plumbers Ltd

The terminal digit system e.g. 10/41/02. This figure is read from right to left and means: drawer no. 2, file no. 41 and document no. 10. This is an extremely accurate system but needs meticulous referencing and may be rather cumbersome to operate.

Other systems combine letters and numbers, e.g. N/03, the letter referring to the alphabetically-ordered file 'N' and the number to the document within that file.

Generally, documents are filed in chronological order with the latest document on top.

Keep filing up-to-date: it's worth the initial extra effort in time-saving and efficiency.

Establish a 'borrowing control system': files removed from storage must be booked out and booked in again.

Confidential files should be kept securely at all times (and this includes confidential computer files).

Don't use paperclips in files – they fall off documents they are intended to hold together and attach themselves randomly to others: use staples.

Company stationery

This is often the first item of expenditure that concerns the new business owner and it is worth spending a little time considering exactly what you need and how to create the best image for your company. The most common items in everyday use are:

Letterhead
Business cards
Compliment slips
Invoices, orders, estimates, quotations, receipts etc.
Printed envelopes
Fax cover sheets

Naturally, what you need will depend largely on the nature of the business, but almost every company should have a professionally printed letterhead, business card and compliment slip. The proliferation of local copyshops, typesetters, printers and suppliers of office stationery in recent years has sharpened up competition considerably and it is worth getting quotes from several before making your choice. The staff will also give advice on layout, design, typefaces and so on. Ask to look at samples of other companies' stationery so you can see what kinds of options are available. If you can afford the services of a design studio then by all means do so, but be prepared for high charges (discuss these before you commission) as well as high quality workmanship.

The general rules for company stationery are:

Quality Buy the best quality paper you can afford and use the same quality on all your stationery.

Colour White is always right. Bright colours can irritate customers and will not photocopy well. Cream and light grey are also acceptable.

Typeface Choose a bold, easy-to-read typeface. Elegant, flowing designs may look attractive but can be difficult to decipher. Colour printing is very much more expensive than black and this extra cost will apply every time you reprint.

Logo Logos are very popular now and can be most effective in 'fixing' a company's image on its customers. Designs can be based on the company's name or initials or can be a small 'icon', such as a tin of paint and a paintbrush for a painter/decorator. A designer can create a logo for you – but be prepared to pay for it!

Avoid unneccesary detail such as borders, rules and flourishes which can appear fussy and unprofessional.

> Every communication from your company to an outsider represents your company's image; make sure it's the right one!

Letterhead

Size: most companies find standard A4 paper (210 x 297 mm) is adequate for everyday purposes. Some firms use printed continuation sheets containing an abbreviated form of the company letterhead. Plain paper of the same weight and colour as the letterhead is a perfectly acceptable alternative.

Information: The letterhead should contain the following:
Name and full postal address of the company
Telephone and fax numbers (including codes)
An indication of the nature of the business (e.g. Painter and Decorator, Management Consultants, Health Studio)
Legal requirements: If your company is a limited company the letterhead must show the registered address and the registration number. (It can also include the names of the directors, but if you choose to do this you must show all the directors' names; this can be expensive if there are likely to be changes). If it is a partnership, the partners' names must be included.

If your company is registered for VAT, the letterhead must include the VAT registration number.

Compliment slips

These are used when sending out information that does not need a full letter, e.g. publicity material, copy of a letter. A standard compliment slip is A7 size and measures 74 x 105mm. It should include:
Company name and full postal address exactly as on the letterhead
Telephone and fax numbers exactly as on the letterhead
The words 'With Compliments', which should be placed so as to leave room for a signature and date or a short message.

If your company sends a large number of standard letters, consider using 'window' envelopes; these can save much time and money.

Business cards

Usually printed on card, these should be no larger than a standard credit card. The business card should show:

Company name and full postal address exactly as on the letterhead

Telephone and fax numbers exactly as on the letterhead

The holder's name, title, telephone extension number and mobile telephone number, if applicable.

Invoices, orders, estimates, quotations, receipts etc.

These should include the same standard name, full postal address, telephone and fax numbers as on the letterhead. The VAT registration number must be shown on the invoices, if applicable. If your company is a registered limited company, invoices, orders, quotations and so on should include the company registration number and directors' names.

Printed envelopes

Envelopes which show the company's name (and address if you so wish, but this is not necessary) are something of a luxury but also carry some prestige.

Fax cover sheets

Again, these are something of a luxury – you can simply type in the necessary information on a letterhead, or create your own fax cover sheet if you have a word processor (see below). If you do decide to invest in a printed fax cover sheet, remember that one fax cover sheet plus one page of text takes twice as long and costs twice as much to send as one page only.

SOME CATERING COMPANY
19 HIGH STREET
ANYTOWN

TEL: 0000 000 0000
FAX: 0000 000 0000

To: From:

Company: Date:

Fax number: Pages to follow:

MESSAGE

Communicating with customers
Letters

Letters are still the basic mode of business communication, in spite of faxes, e-mail and so on. Many people find writing business letters a nerve-wracking and time-consuming occupation, often because they think that there is a special 'formula' of heightened or sophisticated language to which they should adhere. In fact, business communications have been revolutionized over the past few years and the old phrases such as 'yours of the 4th inst' and 'I remain, sir, your obedient servant' have been consigned to history. Today, a good business letter should be SIMPLE, and should be:

Direct and instantly comprehensible
Well-presented
Grammatically correct and without spelling mistakes
Correctly addressed

Keep a good dictionary on your desk and USE IT!

Planning a letter

Most business letters fall into one of the following general categories:
Asking for information
Providing information
Requesting that an action be taken
Apology, complaint, thanks etc.

Consider the category the letter falls into – this is the basis for your letter. Make a list of the points you wish to make and ensure that you have all the information you need. For example, if you are writing to a customer to complain about the non-payment of an invoice, you will need the invoice number, date and details together with the customer name, address, account number.

Look at your list of points and sort them into a logical order, usually putting the most important points first. All letters should have:

An opening: a statement of why you are writing, e.g.
I refer to invoice no.0004321 dated 4 March 1996 in the amount of.....
Thank you for your enquiry about our special Winter Preview advertised in *The Gazette* last week....

Are you concerned about the security of your home?...

The main part: this should set out the principal points of your letter, e.g.
an argument: 'This invoice has now been outstanding for over six months, which, as I am sure you will agree, is an unacceptably long time....'

or

provide information: Enjoy a glass of wine as we present our new Winter Collection which includes...

Our new range of internal and external security systems has been developed to...

The close: the final paragraph should draw a conclusion and make a clear statement of the action the recipient must take, e.g. Unless we receive full settlement of the outstanding amount within 14 days from the date of this letter, we will put the matter in the hands of our solicitors.

The closing date for tickets for our Winter Preview is 30 September and places are limited so call in and make your reservation today. We look forward to seeing you!

If you would like more information or wish to arrange a free, no -obligation survey by one of our Field Managers, then please complete and return the enclosed, reply-paid postcard today.

Keep your letters short and to the point.

Once you have your first draft completed, look it over once or twice and check any doubtful spellings. Make sure the name and address of the recipient are correct and you have remembered to put in the date. If the letter is complicated and/or very important, it is a good idea to leave the first draft for a few hours and then re-read it with a fresh eye. In this way any thoughts you have had in the meantime can be added, for example, or you may choose to re-phrase or omit certain parts.

Now you can type the final version. Read it through very carefully and make sure you have an accurate copy. Don't forget to add any enclosures before sealing the envelope.

Layout

The trend today is towards clean, clear text using open punctuation (i.e. no punctuation at all, except in the body of the letter) and fully-blocked style (see example on page 187). However the traditional punctuation and paragraph indentation are also acceptable (see sample on page 188). Once you have chosen a style you like then make that your 'house style' and use it consistently.

All business letters should contain:
Letterhead
Letter reference (such as initials of person dictating and person typing the letter; number of file)
Date
Name and address of recipient
Salutation
Subject heading
Body of letter
Complimentary close
Signature
Sender's name and designation (i.e. position in company)

NEVER be abusive or use bad language in a letter or on the telephone. It is always unconstructive and you may come to regret it if the dispute becomes a legal matter.

The Eagle Hotel
Main Road
Eaglesthorpe
Shropshire SH4 6BX
Tel: 0000 000 0000
Fax: 0000 000 0000

Mrs P Williamson
The Flower Shop
43 High Street
Eaglesthorpe
Shropshire SH4 5BX

Your ref: PW/ES/14
Our ref: RP/MC/Banq.Flow.

14 December 1996

Dear Mrs Williamson

Contract for Supply of Flowers for Christmas Period

(paragraph one)

(paragraph two)

Yours sincerely

Robert Partridge
Banqueting Manager

NEVER allow any letter to leave the office without making a copy.

The telephone

Every communication that is made between your company and an external recipient can enhance or detract from your company's image. This applies especially to telephone communications. No matter how harassed or irritated you (or your caller!) might be, you MUST be patient, polite and helpful. Here are some general tips:

Always keep a notepad and pen by the telephone; 'Just hold on a tick while I get a pencil' does little to enhance your professional image.

Always answer a call by giving your company name and/or your own name and an approriate greeting (Good Morning, Good Afternoon); NEVER just say 'Hallo' or, even worse, 'Yes?' or 'Yeah?'

Take the caller's name and number.

If you need to put the caller on hold, then say this is what you are doing and never leave a caller for longer than 40 seconds without coming back to him/her and explaining the reason for the wait. Give the caller the option of holding, calling back or leaving a message.

Make sure that messages you take are delivered promptly and accurately to the appropriate person.

Always try to help the caller – your company's image depends on it.

If you use a telephone answering machine, ensure that the

message you leave is straightforward and that you always deal with incoming messages promptly on your return.

When you make a business call yourself, always give your name and company name and explain the reason for your call at the outset; think about what you are going to say before you pick up the phone – this will help you to sound efficient and to speak precisely and with confidence.

If you work from home, make sure your family can answer the telephone properly – your business may depend on it.

DON'T SAY	*DO* SAY
Who did you say?	I'm sorry, I didn't quite catch your name.
Haven't a clue when he'll be back. Sorry.	I'm not sure when he'll be back. Can I take a message?
It's nothing to do with me.	Could I take your number and I'll get someone to call you back?
We don't do that.	This isn't really in our field, but you could try ...

SAMPLE LETTER – FULLY BLOCKED STYLE

2 The Cottages
Green Lane
London SW24 8NG

21 August 1996

The Manager
Devonshire Bank
12 Market Street
Henton GV22 6DE

Dear Sir

Business Account

As you may know, I would like set up my own catering company.
Could I arrange a meeting with you or one of your Business Advisers
to discuss the possibility of opening a Business Account? I would also
like to discuss the Devonshire Bank Personal Pension Plan.

I would appreciate an early appointment.

Yours faithfully

T. Baker

SAMPLE LETTER – SEMI-BLOCKED STYLE

15 The Elms
Braunton
GS22 4HB

26th June 1996

Mrs J. Pickford,
The Manager,
Derryvale Hotel,
16 Holgate Street,
Derryvale,
DV2 7KG

Dear Mrs Pickford,

<u>Reservation</u>

Following our telephone conversation earlier today, please would you reserve a double room for my husband and me, for Friday 19th July to Sunday 21st July inclusive (2 nights bed and breakfast).

I understand the cost will be £40 per night, breakfast included.

I am enclosing a cheque for £20 as a non-refundable deposit against cancellation.

I look forward to meeting you.

Yours sincerely,

E. Bloggs (Mrs)
Enc.

Time management and avoiding stress

As a self-employed person you have almost total control over the hours you work and the temptations to start late, catch up on the daily paper, take long coffee breaks and long lunches are very strong. Reserve these pleasures for when your business is a resounding success. In the meantime a little thought now on how you manage your time can only benefit your business.

Identifying Priorities

In a new business, generating sales and finding customers is usually a top priority, so most of your time will be spent in this way. Careful planning here can save you so much time in the future. Use a diary to note down any holidays, special occasions or forthcoming events. You can then plan around these. Next, on a weekly or monthly basis, decide on your targets and divide these into three sections: *Essential*, *Urgent* and *If Possible* categories.

Essential: these tasks might include invoicing current sales, arranging sales appointments, putting an advertisement in the local paper.
Urgent: tasks in this category might be investigating the cost and need for new equipment (new software for the computer, for example, or a new van).
If Possible: this final category could include contacting the local Chamber of Commerce for some information, checking stationery supplies, arranging for a minor repair to equipment.

Using your diary, pencil in times allocated to these tasks and organize your week/month in the most practical and time-efficient way. If possible avoid making appointments in the town centre early in the morning when rush-hour traffic will be at its worst and you will lose time. Take the train if possible - you can work while you're travelling and will avoid the frustration and time-wasting involved in trying to find a parking space.

At the end of each week or month you can then look back at your list of objectives and see how many you achieved. You will also be able to see whether or not your list accurately reflected the needs of the business and can take this into account when listing the next set of objectives. The 'If Possible' tasks from the previous period may now have become 'Urgent' for example, and you can see this at a glance. You may see that you spent too much time on certain tasks which did not give the results you hoped for and can readjust your approach to these. For example, you may feel that you spent too much unproductive time on individual sales calls and may now decide to set yourself a maximum time for such calls. Reassess your priorities constantly, adapt and make changes in the light of experience; don't get stuck in a rut.

No matter how logical and efficient you make the day-to-day running of your business, there will always be certain aspects that you enjoy much more than others. Capitalize on these as far as possible because you will not only gain more satisfaction from your work but will be more productive when doing those things. Clearly it will be impossible in a one man/one woman business to avoid the more onerous and mundane tasks, but it is worthwhile considering ways of maximizing the time you spend working on aspects of the business that you enjoy. As with your weekly or monthly objectives, reassess the situation from time to time as the company progresses.

Consider the following points (making a list might help clarify these):

What parts of your work do you enjoy most and what are you best at?

How do these fit in with your targets?

Which aspects of your work do you dislike?

Which parts of your work could be delegated?

For example, if you enjoy making contacts, going out and about and meeting people, making sales and so on, but loathe staying in the office answering queries and sending out invoices, then you might consider taking on some help, even on a part-time basis, or perhaps freelance help from someone who works at home (calls can be automatically diverted from one number to another when you are absent). You may be unsure at first whether you should commit yourself to this kind of expenditure, but remember that if your company depends on generating sales, and this is your strength, then you are best employed making sales and paying someone else to type up invoices and keep the accounts. On the other hand you may feel your strength lies in organization and administration and you don't really like face-to-face customer contact. Why not take on an experienced, self-employed salesman or saleswoman (perhaps on a commission-only basis at the beginning) who can make the contacts while you organize the follow-up?

As your business progresses, constantly reassess the way you use your time, and readjust as necessary, spending as much time as you reasonably can on priority tasks. Below are some general guidelines:

- Keep regular working hours as far as possible.
- Set sensible targets for yourself and any others who work for you.
- Keep meetings as short as possible.
- Learn to delegate.
- Keep routine paperwork under control. If you can't afford to delegate this, then set aside a regular time to deal with it (preferably not on a Friday afternoon!), grit your teeth and bear it. Do not allow it to build up to unmanageable proportions.

Occasional crises are unavoidable, but if you are lurching from crisis to crisis you must completely overhaul your method of working and start to PRIORITIZE.

> Time management is the key to efficiency.

Guidelines for effective delegation

- Explain to the person exactly what is to be accomplished.
- Make it absolutely clear how much authority the person has to decide on how to deal with the matter; or is he/she to follow your own methods/instructions exactly?
- Be precise about completion date, budget and so on.
- How frequently do you want the person to report back to you on progress? And in what way?
- Once you have delegated a task KEEP OUT OF THE WAY and DON'T WORRY!

Dealing with stress

Although the temptation to start late and take long lunches may be hard to resist, the other side of the self-employed coin is, of course, overwork leading to stress. A certain amount of stress is unavoidable in any walk of life and can even be beneficial – excited anticipation of meeting a challenge, for example, results in heightened awareness and a burst of energy, leading to the feeling of wellbeing. On the other hand, constant and long-term pressure can have serious effects on your health, your relationships and on the quality of your work. The symptoms of stress have been exhaustively documented in recent years and vary from the physical, such as headaches, ulcers, skin conditions and fatigue, to the behavioural, such as a constant short-temper, frustration, inability to concentrate and loss of perspective. Work problems include the need to take work home in the evenings and weekends on a regular basis, refusal to take holidays, failure to meet targets and deadlines, lack of organization.

Be aware of the signs of long-term stress; if you recognize these in yourself or your colleagues you must take the time to discuss the problems causing the situation and make changes to overcome them (see above, *Time Management*). Below are some general guidelines on avoiding stress:

- Take the time to prioritize and plan ahead.
- Take normal holidays and days off without feeling guilty – you deserve it!
- If you are struggling with some aspects of your business, for example using the computer or book-keeping, employ someone to take over or go on a training course.
- Eat properly and take exercise; taking the stairs instead of the lift is a valuable cardio-vascular exercise. Try not to stay in the office all day - go out for a walk at lunchtime.
- Get adequate sleep. Do not work late regularly or take work home at weekends.
- Spend time with family and friends; take up an interest that has no connection with your business.

Long-term stress can lead to serious illness.

Working from home

Many newly self-employed people work, at least initially, from home – the advantages are self-evident – and with the coming of ever more sophisticated electronic communications and information systems (word processors, faxes, e-mail, cable television and so on) these numbers are likely to grow in the future. And though it may be no problem at all to leave those long rush-hour queues behind, it may not be quite so easy to find the self-discipline needed to work successfully from home. Below are some suggestions which may help:

- Keep regular 'office hours'; start work at the same time every day and give yourself regular breaks, just as if you were working for an employer.
- Don't be tempted to work long hours on a regular basis just because it's easy to do so. Keep your working day within defined limits and leave time for leisure interests.
- If possible, assign a room as your 'office' and make sure other members of the household know that when you are in your 'office' you are not to be interrupted. (If you plan to dedicate a room in your house totally for business purposes, however, you may find it has implications for Capital Gains Tax when the property is sold. Try to keep some domestic belongings in it to show a dual purpose or at least be aware of possible future problems.)
- Install a telephone extension in your workspace so that you do not need to leave your desk to answer the telephone.
- Dress as if you were going out to work – you will feel more efficient and it will help to mark the division between working time and leisure time.
- If you live alone and work from home you can come to feel very isolated; make sure you spend time with friends and colleagues – even a telephone call can help!

2. MONEY MATTERS
Tax

Until recently there was no legal requirement for the self-employed to keep records for Income Tax purposes (although companies registered for VAT were required to keep appropriate records, along with limited companies and company directors). Now, however, the 1994 Finance Act stipulates that certain trading records must be kept. Failure to keep adequate records can result in substantial fines. Naturally, the precise nature of the records you need to keep depends on the size and type of your business, but it will always involve three key elements:

1. Setting up an adequate system of recording business transactions.
2. Maintaining them scrupulously and keeping them up-to-date.
3. Retaining them for as long as required (a minimum of six years).

> All businesses pay tax – but how you pay tax depends on what type of business you run. Business decisions can have tax implications, so think about your tax position from the start; consult a business counsellor or your accountant for the best advice.

What do you need to keep?

In simple terms, you must keep a record of every receipt and every payment that takes place in the course of your day-to-day business life. At your annual account date this will include:

- the takings
- all items of expenditure (e.g. rent, rates, electricity, insurances, repairs, vehicle running expenses, wages and salaries, stationery, National Insurance contributions, telephone, postage etc.)
- any private money that is taken into the business and where it comes from
- money taken out of the business bank account for private purposes and the reason (e.g. life insurance premiums)
- market value of any goods taken from the business for your own private use, unless you paid the full retail price
- full details of amounts owed to you by customers
- full details of amounts owed by you to suppliers
- an annual record of stock and/or work in progress

To help with the preparation of your accounts you must keep:

- all bank and building society statements
- cheque stubs, paying-in books, receipted bills, sales invoices etc.
- records of your personal and building society accounts, especially if money is transferred between the business account and your private account

Unless you have some experience in managing accounts, you should seriously consider employing an accountant to advise you. However, it is up to you to keep accurate and detailed records, whether or not you have an accountant: the responsibility is yours.

> Regular, orderly and accurate record-keeping is essential for a business to succeed. Stick to a strict regime for your paperwork. Remember that the Inland Revenue and Customs and Excise may require sight of your records at short notice - a well-organized record-keeping system NOW could save you time and money later.

Setting up an adequate system of business transactions

For most small businesses a CASH BOOK (to record all bank transactions, cash receipts, payments and withdrawals), supplemented by a PETTY CASH BOOK to record simple transactions (such as buying stamps, typewriter ribbons) will be sufficient.

If you are running a larger business, your accountant can advise you on what records to keep.

These records are used at the end of your tax year to support the figures in your tax returns. It cannot be emphasized too strongly that IT IS IN YOUR OWN INTERESTS to make sure your records are kept up-to-date and are accurate.

If you decide to keep your records on computer, instead of using a cash book, you must still keep the original receipts, bank books etc. to support them, unless you use an optical imaging system or microfilm the original documents. Remember to make regular back-ups on floppy disks or tape in case your system 'crashes' and you lose all the data stored on the hard disk – it DOES happen!

It is helpful to visit a Tax Enquiry Centre BEFORE you start your business. Staff can guide you through the various rules and implications of the new Self-Assessment tax system and also offer advice on how to pay your own tax and National Insurance contributions. As your business develops and you need to start employing staff, the Tax Enquiry Centre officers can assist in showing you how to calculate wages for employees and deduct tax and National Insurance from their pay. It's a good idea to obtain a contact name in your local Enquiry Centre - this means that each time you telephone or visit the office you can speak to the same officer, who will know you and already have a knowledge of your business.

Self-assessment

From April 1997 a new system of self-assessment will be introduced by the Inland Revenue. This new system applies to everyone, including the self-employed. A new-style tax return will be sent to all self-employed people which will combine all your sources of income, gains, reliefs, deductions and allowances for the tax year. You can calculate your own tax payable on the basis of these figures or the Inland Revenue will do it for you. A clear statement of your tax situation will then be issued, so you will know exactly what your tax position is. Contact your local Tax Enquiry Centre (in the telephone book under Inland Revenue) for leaflets and brochures which explain, in simple terms, just how this will work. Advisers at your local Tax Enquiry Centre are available for personal consultation and can help with free, confidential advice on various aspects of setting up in business. Most offices are open on weekdays from 10 00 to 16 00.

Robert Dallas, an accountant, says:

My experience of people who are setting up in business for the first time is that they are very concerned about Income Tax and want to know how the Income Tax system will apply to their business. However, they often don't consider Value Added Tax, merely assuming that they can charge VAT and recover VAT and that it is really a fairly simple tax. This is far from the case as VAT can often be a minefield for the new business.

I would therefore recommend that you discuss fully with your accountant how VAT applies to your business, how you are going to maintain the records that you need to satisfy the VAT authorities and also what other impact VAT might have as far as you are concerned.

VAT (Value Added Tax)

At the time of writing, if the taxable turnover of your business is more than £47,000 in any 12 month period, you must register to pay VAT. Your local VAT office can give you information on what business transactions are exempt or zero-rated for VAT. In all other cases VAT is chargeable at the full rate, currently 17.5%. This means, basically, that once you are registered for VAT you must add 17.5% to all the invoices you send to your customers. Invoices and credit notes will show your VAT number which will be given to you when you register. You will also be charged VAT by your suppliers (if they are registered for VAT themselves), whether or not you are registered for VAT. VAT paid by you to your suppliers is known as the input tax; VAT paid to you by your customers is known as the output tax. Every three months you complete a VAT tax form sent to you by Customs and Excise. Input tax is subtracted from output tax and the return is sent back with a cheque for the VAT payable by you. If the input tax is greater than the output tax, you can reclaim the difference from Customs and Excise. Full details and advice can be found at your local VAT office (look under Customs & Excise in the telephone directory).

If you are in any doubt at all that you may be liable to pay VAT then you are strongly advised to contact the VAT department at your local Customs and Excise office. THERE ARE SEVERE PENALTIES FOR NOT REGISTERING

Once you are registered for VAT you may be able to reclaim the VAT paid on goods and services you bought for setting up the business before you registered.

National Insurance

As a self-employed person you will pay flat-rate, weekly, Class 2 National Insurance contributions. (There are some exceptions e.g. people on low earnings, men over 65 and women over 60, people under 16 years of age; check with your local Department of Social Security if in doubt.) You may also be liable to pay earnings-related Class 4 National Insurance contributions depending on how much profit your business makes. The easiest way to pay Class 2 National Insurance contributions is by monthly direct debit.

If you are unsure how much you should be paying, contact your local DSS office where you will be able to get advice on what you need to pay, when and how. In any case you MUST advise the DSS of your change of situation – from employed or unemployed to self-employed. Quote your National Insurance number when you telephone or write.

Failure to pay National Insurance contributions can have serious implications for future state benefits and pensions. IGNORE THE RULES AT YOUR OWN RISK.

If you are employing staff you are responsible for collecting income tax and National Insurance from their earnings before they are paid. See Section 3, *Employing People*, for more information

If you work for an employer AND run your own business, you may have to pay Class 1 (from your employment), Class 2 and Class 4 National Insurance contributions depending on how much you earn. Just because you are paying one class of contributions does not exempt you from paying another.

3. EMPLOYING PEOPLE

Depending on the size and nature of your business, you may need to employ people from the outset. Employing people is a considerable responsibility and should be given a good deal of careful thought.

Your employees can be one of your company's greatest assets – or one of its greatest liabilities.

Recruitment
1. The job
Draw up a job description. State simply and clearly what the work involves. Apart from being a useful basis for the future

employer/employee relationship, it will help you to clarify, in your own mind, precisely the areas where you need help.

2. The conditions
Here you should consider:
Salary: how much; paid weekly, monthly?
Hours: how many per week; meal breaks; overtime
Holidays: how many days per year (in addition to statutory holidays)

If you are not sure what the current conditions are for the kind of work you have in mind, contact your local JobCentre, trade association or your local ACAS (Advisory, Conciliation and Arbitration Service) office.

3. Advertising
Draw up an advertisement and place it in your local JobCentre and/or in your local paper. Professional posts are usually advertised in one of the more important regional papers or national dailies.

You must not make any distinction on grounds of race or gender in your advertisement. (There are, however, certain exceptions to the general rules on sex discrimination (e.g. personal services). If you are in doubt then it is worthwhile checking before you advertise the job.) Recent moves also indicate that specifying a maximum age will also become prohibited in the future.

4. Selecting and interviewing

Read the applications carefully. Look out for 'danger areas' such as frequent job changes, complaints about former employers. Read 'between the lines' and trust your instincts. What about handwriting, spelling and presentation? If the applicant does not pay much attention to these, in such an important exercise as applying for a job, then he/she is unlikely to pursue high standards of commitment once the job is theirs. If appropriate, ask candidates to bring their certificates or other evidence of training with them; it saves time later.

Think about some key questions to ask each applicant. Write down the answers if you are interviewing several people – it will help to remind you later.

Present the job simply and clearly to the candidate; be honest about such issues as prospects, promotion, skills needed and so on. During the interview consider how you are responding to the candidate – after all, you will have to work with him/her on a daily basis. This is particularly vital in a small firm.

Be diligent about chasing up references and confirming qualifications – people often lie.

Once you have chosen, write a letter to the candidate offering the job. Remember, the letter becomes legally binding once the job is accepted, so be careful with the wording.

> If you have any doubts at all about a candidate, no matter how vague, then do not appoint him or her.

Conditions of employment

At the time of writing, if someone works for you for more than 16 hours a week they have certain rights. You should check if these rules now apply to part-time workers as there is considerable pressure to provide greater statutory protection for people who work fewer than 16 hours a week.

Contract of Employment

An employee must receive, within 13 weeks of his or her starting date, a written statement of the main terms and conditions of employment. This should include:

- name of employer and employee
- job title
- starting date of employment
- working hours, including overtime arrangements if applicable
- rate of pay, when payable and by what method
- statement of benefits, such as pension scheme (where applicable), sick pay
- holiday entitlement
- length of notice to be given (by both employer and employee) to terminate employment
- disciplinary and grievance procedures.

A sample Contract of Employment is given in the Appendix.

Statutory rights

The Employment Protection (Consolidation) Act 1978, Race Relations Act 1976 and Sex Discrimination Act 1975 have established certain fundamental rights for employees. Among these are the right to:

- be given a minimum period of notice for their term of employment and to be given clear, written reasons for the termination of their employment. If an employee has worked in the same company for two years or more, this includes the right not to be dismissed unfairly (after two years an employee can take the employer to an Industrial Tribunal on the grounds of unfair dismissal)
- receive Statutory Sick Pay (up to 28 weeks); maternity pay and maternity leave and the right to return to work if certain criteria are met
- equal pay for work of equal value
- equal treatment and not to be discriminated against on grounds of gender, race or marital status
- take part in trade union activities
- receive redundancy pay after two years employment in the same company and to continued employment under the same conditions if the business is sold as a going concern.

Employment legislation is complex; ask your JobCentre for help if in doubt. ACAS offers a free, confidential helpline.

Health and safety

The Health and Safety At Work Act 1974 and the Offices, Shops and Railways Act 1963 are the major sources for health and safety legislation.

The responsibility for the welfare of the company's workers and those affected by the company's activities lies principally with the employer, although employees also have a duty to protect themselves and their co-workers. The 1969 Employer's Liability (Compulsory Insurance) Act requires employers to insure themselves against accidents and injury at work and to display a current certificate of insurance where employees can see it.

Basically the law requires the employer to provide a clean, safe workplace with adequate space, heating, lighting and toilet facilities. Machinery should be adequately maintained and safe to operate and relevant employees should be trained and supervised in the operation of the machinery. Fire precautions should be taken and First Aid facilities provided. If you employ more than five people you must prepare a formal statement of policy on health and safety at work and put this policy into practice. You do not need to do this if you employ fewer than five people, but the law still requires you to fulfil the obligations of care contained in the legislation.

The local office of the Health and Safety Executive can answer any questions you may have (and if you are setting up a manufacturing business you should talk to them at an early stage as the regulations controlling chemicals, effluent and so on are rigorous). You can obtain copies of the Acts from HMSO (Her Majesty's Stationery Office) through good bookshops, and the Health and Safety Executive publishes its own booklet,

What You Should Know, available from HSE Information Centre, Broad Lane, Sheffield S3 7HQ; telephone 0541 545500.

Pay-As-You-Earn (PAYE) Income Tax and National Insurance

Income tax

You are responsible for deducting income tax (PAYE) from your employees' earnings before they receive them. At the time of writing, PAYE must be applied to anyone currently earning more than £72.90 per week. If you do not deduct the appropriate amounts, then you may be required to pay the tax yourself plus any penalties.

Once you have decided to appoint an employee, contact your local tax office or Tax Enquiry Centre. They will send you a leaflet which explains what you must do, plus a New Employer's Starter Pack. Remember, the tax office is there to help you – getting it right from the start will avoid costly mistakes and time-consuming problems.

If you are employing part-timers then check their PAYE status carefully. Even if they earn below the limits for PAYE and National Insurance with you, they may have other sources of income (another job, pension etc.) and thus be over the limits. YOU may then be required to pay the tax and National Insurance owing, whether or not you have deducted it from your employee's salary, together with any possible penalties.

National Insurance

National Insurance contributions must be made, currently by both employer and employee where the employee earns more than £59 per week. It is your responsibility, as employer, to ensure this is paid. The New Employer's Starter Pack mentioned above also explains how to operate National Insurance contributions and provides an introduction to how Statutory Maternity Pay and Statutory Sick Pay are operated.

Employees are entitled to receive a statement with their pay showing details of payment and deductions made.

Casual labour is defined as employing a person to work on a single job for a specified period. If this arrangement extends to include regular work, e.g. one day a week, it is no longer casual and other regulations apply.

Discipline, complaints and termination of employment

Even in the best-regulated and friendliest offices, problems and disputes occasionally arise, and it is best to deal with these as soon as they occur to avoid crises which can only damage the business.

It is always helpful to have a clear and recognized procedure for channelling disciplinary problems and complaints, and a copy of this should be given to each employee. If, as employer, you follow these rules consistently and fairly, you will minimize disruption to the company's activities and it will also reduce the risk of an employee taking out an action for unfair dismissal. The 1978 Employment Protection (Consolidation) Act provides that an employer can be justified in terminating employment if:

(i) There is a 'fair' reason for dismissal
(ii) The employer is acting reasonably in deciding to dismiss the employee.

'Fair' reasons

Some of the 'fair' reasons include:

- capability (the employee cannot do the job properly because, for example, he/she does not have the qualifications or is ill on a long term basis)
- conduct (the employee has been fighting, drinking to excess, stealing)
- redundancy
- contravention of a statutory duty or restriction (losing a driving licence, for example)
- other substantial reasons (a criminal conviction, for instance)

'Fair' procedures

The employer must show that he/she has acted 'reasonably' in dismissing the employee for a particular reason. This means that:

- the procedure must be 'fair'; i.e. the employee was allowed to state his/her case

- it must be reasonable, in the circumstances, to dismiss the employee. For example, was the employee warned that his/her conduct was unacceptable and might lead to dismissal?

The Advisory, Conciliation and Arbitration Service (ACAS) issues a Code of Practice on disciplinary procedures which offers good advice on establishing the rules and procedures for complaints and discipline.

An employee can bring an action for wrongful dismissal (for example, if the employer is in breach of contract) without a continuous period of service; an action for unfair dismissal can, generally, only be raised if the employee has been in continuous service for a period of two years. Employers can take out employer's protection insurance which covers against expenses and compensation if the company is taken to an industrial tribunal.

'Conduct' is the commonest reason given for dismissal.

CASE HISTORY
Mark, owner of hairdressing salon

I worked for several years for a local hairdressing company which owned several salons, eventually becoming a Director. Although I was well-paid and had a high-powered and reasonably secure position, I knew I could go no further with the company. I began to think about setting up my own business.

Because I'd had a good deal of experience dealing with the organizational and financial side of the business in my job, I knew what I was doing and risks I was taking.

I started in my present salon about five years ago, but it's only fairly recently that I've seen a real profit, and that's only 10-12%. And even so I've worked seven days a week – although I now force myself to take a day off, for my own good! I had hoped to open another salon by now, but the business was subject to a 2 1/2 year income tax investigation. Although I cooperated fully and there were no real problems, the investigation cost me about £10,000 to defend and countless sleepless nights. I have always been meticulous about keeping my records up-to-date and this helped me a great deal during the investigation.

Would I become self-employed again? Yes, because I like controlling my own working life and I enjoy seeing young people coming in and training and maturing into competent, skilled stylists – that gives me great satisfaction. My advice to anyone thinking of running their own business would be to be prepared to work very hard; to get the right financial and legal advice before starting (and be prepared to pay for it) and be rigorous about keeping all your records really up-to-date and complete.

PART FOUR

STAYING
IN
BUSINESS!

STAYING IN BUSINESS!

Tell them what you're going to tell them   (The beginning)
Tell them   (The middle)
Tell them what you've told them   (The end)

This was the maxim that we said was the effective way of getting your message across, and we intend to apply it ourselves. This last section is intended to be a reminder for you of all the key aspects of how to set up and run an effective small (or possibly not so small) business. We hope that we have summarized matters for you in a way that will stick in your mind, but the whole book is designed to be used for your reference whenever you need a reminder or a prompt in any area. Within this section we draw upon practical experience gained in a broad spectrum of business, to bring to you a range of 'insider' tips which can be applied to almost any field you are considering.

Borrow money when you don't actually need it

Bank managers are famous for lending you an umbrella when it's sunny, and asking for it back when it starts to rain! Give your bank manager a chance to see how reliable a customer you are BEFORE you get to the desperate stage! As you will soon learn, there's no point in going along to see your friendly local bank manager when you're strapped for cash, because at that point you'll be classified as a very high risk. It is better gradually to build up your credit rating by borrowing relatively small amounts in the medium term for assets such as vehicles which are generally pretty easy to finance, providing that they're not old and well past their best. For example, you might want to acquire a small car or van. Even if you have enough spare cash to purchase it outright (sorry, ESPECIALLY if you have enough!), ask your manager to provide 80 to 90% of the price over a two or three year period at the best rate you can negotiate. Your rationale will be that you can then keep your cash in reserve for any unforeseen expenses or shortfall in income. (In fact, you will probably find that this does indeed turn out to be the case, and you'll be glad that you did it this way.)

Talk to your accountant often

Accountants frequently have the image of being people who simply re-hash the book-keeping work that you've been doing painstakingly for a year, present you eventually with a set of accounts which take the wind out of your sails, and a bill which leaves you speechless. While it would be difficult to deny that there could be a certain element of truth in each of these points, this would probably be due to a lack of regular contact with your chosen accountant. It can be difficult to find time to think about much more than simply surviving the day-to-day battles which inevitably occupy and possibly eventually dominate the entrepreneur's daily agenda, but your accountant can be a marvellous source of comfort, support and assistance if you have a good working relationship. If you find yourself with a problem over VAT, PAYE, NI or any other matter which involves dealing with bureaucracy, your accountant is the ideal comrade-in-arms. He will be used to dealing with these people over a long period, and is probably better mentally equipped to deal with your problems, since he is not emotionally involved in your business the way that you are.

Choose your staff carefully

One of the great temptations in business is to employ people that you know and think you can trust simply because they happen to be available. While it is true that you have to be able to get along well with your staff, this method of recruitment can be fraught with problems, such as:

- You risk offending your employed friend or family when you have to sack them due to either incompetence or lack of work for them – either way you could be portrayed as the villain of the piece, and would find yourself in a no-win situation. It CAN work but ...

- You might feel uncomfortable with someone you know being privy to inside information about how well – or how badly – your business is doing.

Whether or not you intend to employ family or friends, you owe it to your business to be as professional as you can be in staff selection. After all, if you are looking for someone that you can get along with, who can be trusted, and whose qualifications and experience closely match your requirements, you will hope that they will stay with you in the long term, and that you can rely on them to help you make the business successful.

If you are inexperienced in staff selection, consider using an outside agency, possibly the local job-centre whose senior staff are usually highly experienced in this kind of work, to help you draw up a job specification and a possible employee profile. If you are going to advertise the post yourself, this will help you avoid attracting applications from people who are not suitable, and save you a lot of time and heartache in the early stages of selection. This information will allow you to compare your requirements with the curriculum vitae of applicants, and draw up your list of possible and probable candidates.

Don't employ – deploy!

It might seem like a strange suggestion, but would it be worth considering setting up some of your staff in their own business? If they form a unit which is self-contained and which could be supplying the same or similar service to yours and other businesses without affecting yours adversely, it might be worth considering hiving off this operation and shifting the burden of responsibility for this aspect of your business. You might even become aware of rumblings within the ranks of the desire to 'do their own thing'. Take advantage of this energy and motivation and positively encourage independence. You will already have noticed that there is no one in your business who is going to work as hard as you, in other words the person who works for himself or herself! By allowing your staff to become owner/managers themselves you will have unleashed a powerful force which can then be turned to your advantage – remember that while you employ these staff YOU are responsible for all their mistakes, delays, holidays, sickness leave, wages, overtime, lost time and down time – let THEM have the pleasure if this is what will motivate them and provide you with the service that you need at a fair price. The main difference is that you are now able to control the unit cost of your purchases of the article or service. You are able to dictate terms of price, payment and quality, and it's up to them to sink or swim by their own efforts. You might even rent them factory or other space, as well as selling or renting them your old equipment to get started.

The key to doing this successfully is to be acutely aware of exactly what business you are in. Remember that earlier in the book we discussed how it wasn't the manufacture of a product or service but its sale that generated the real profit. Look at Marks and Spencer's operation. They are suppliers of goods to a retail market which they know intimately. They have effective control over a significant number of manufacturers who are geared up to meeting their exacting quality standards, but the risk in the manufacturing process does not belong to M&S – the manufacturers and suppliers still have to fund their own business, and negotiate whatever terms they can with the high street retailer to make it worth their while. Which party would you rather be in this case?

Don't expect too much of Homo sapiens

You may be one of these fortunate people who have a natural ability to get the most out of everyone they meet, including staff, suppliers and customers. But don't think that everyone that you encounter will have the same exacting high standards as you, whether relating to service, quality control or morality in business. When dealing with human beings, one useful maxim might be 'Expect the worst and hope for the best.' That way, you won't be disappointed too often.

It is amazing to think that in these days when the economy is said to be in the doldrums, and businesses are supposedly fighting it out for every last available pound in the customer's pocket, it seems like an almost impossible task to get two independent firms in the building trade to provide you with an estimate within a week for what should be a profitable job such as repairs following burst pipes in the attic! Why is this? It is impossible to say exactly, but it would appear that the general levels of service within the building industry leave much to be desired. Anyone wishing to carry on a business within the industry, with a reputation for efficient and caring service, must surely have a major opportunity in front of them.

Try to confirm Terms of Reference (specification or objectives) clearly in writing before starting a job.

This lets YOU know what you're letting yourself in for in a particular job. Obviously, this can be difficult or even impossible in some instances, such as hairdressing, but it can save your business credibility (at least!) in other situations. You can avoid being taken advantage of by others by making sure that you have stated the objectives of the contract before commencement, and getting the other party to agree to them or amending them as necessary. Remember that there are some people who seem to make a living out of getting work done and then refusing to pay on the grounds that it wasn't what you were asked to do. This applies to certain unsavoury individuals as well as to businesses, and if you're not careful you could end up a victim by getting started quickly in order to please the customer, mistakenly thinking that everything will turn out satisfactorily in the end. Generally speaking, customers will avoid paying you - if you allow them to.

State your terms of business clearly BEFORE you begin a new job or contract.

This lets the customers know what THEY are letting themselves in for when dealing with you. This is closely related to the Terms of Reference mentioned above, but can be a standard set of conditions which you apply to each new contract. You can get assistance from a lawyer to formalise the terms of contract, but it helps the professionals greatly if you have a fair idea of what you want to achieve. This allows them to ensure that they are providing you with the most appropriate contract for the intended purpose. You might be pleasantly surprised to find that your legal adviser is able to call upon a wealth of practical experience in your chosen field, and this can be a great comfort. Try to make sure that the language used is as clear and uncomplicated as possible, to allow the customer to have confidence in your business methods. If possible, make sure that each customer provides you with a written order which confirms that they accept your standard terms and conditions, which can be incorporated into the one form quite easily by your solicitor. Give the customer a copy of these, along with the Terms of Reference for the job and a covering letter confirming start dates etc. as applicable. In some instances, you will have to accept the terms and conditions set by a customer in order to get a contract, especially in the building industry, but do not be afraid to ask your lawyer to advise you on the acceptability of the terms proposed, or to ask for certain terms to be waived or modified if you think them too onerous. If you can't find business on terms broadly acceptable to you, don't take on the job. It's far better to have avoided a potentially dangerous situation than to try to fight your way back from the brink when it all goes wrong.

Don't pay bills too soon!

In your eagerness to create a good impression with your suppliers, you might be tempted to settle their accounts as soon as you receive them – don't! As time goes on, you'll appreciate that it is better to conserve your cash for those unforeseen circumstances and unexpected bills that have an unfortunate habit of cropping up out of the blue. When you enter into a contract with a supplier, they will have agreed to a certain period of credit before the payment falls due. YOU might want payment on delivery or with the order, but your customers will have other ideas. The most common terms expected nowadays are generally called 30 days' credit. However, this doesn't mean 30 days from the date of supply or from the date of invoice, but 30 days from the end of the month in which the invoice is raised. As a supplier of goods or services, this can sorely dent your cash flow if allowed (especially when customers try to push it to 60 or even 90 days), but as a customer it can have benefits for your cash flow, since you effectively have nearly two months credit if ordering and taking delivery on the 1st of the month. There is usually no interest penalty for settling bills at the end of the full 30-day credit period, so by leaving your money in the bank or on overnight deposit you can earn additional profits. Of course, you might want to use your financial strength to negotiate additional discounts for early settlement of purchase invoices, even if the possibility is not mentioned on suppliers' invoices. You will generally find that your suppliers would be delighted at the prospect of improving their cash flow, and are prepared to discuss discounts in excess of the interest you might have earned by leaving the money in the bank. If this seems strange to you, it is simply because you have yet to suffer from the enormous problems which can be created by late payment of accounts. If you are careful you might never have to learn the hard way. Whatever terms you agree, put them clearly in writing, but do not expect all (or even any!) of your customers to respect them.

Another reason for not paying bills too soon (especially for no financial benefit) is that your suppliers will certainly notice it when you find that you cannot settle up as soon as previously, thanks to late receipt of payments due to yourself. Even though you might then simply be falling into step with everyone else, the adverse effect that this can have in someone's confidence in your business can be out of proportion to the true position. Since business is all about confidence, you might start off the rumour machine which itself could eventually bring your business to the grinding halt that everyone imagined!

Don't pay bills too late!

It's all very well taking the maximum amount of credit that you are offered by suppliers, but remember that you are trying to build up relationships based on mutual trust. If you abuse their generous terms you will adversely affect your credit rating with them. When you go to open another credit account with a new supplier, you will be asked to provide at least two references from existing suppliers. If you have not settled your account regularly within their normal terms of trade, this factual information will be passed on truthfully, and the potential new supplier may decline to provide you with the credit account you seek. If you have a good record of payment with your suppliers, it becomes all the more noticeable when you unilaterally decide to extend their credit terms to you. Avoid this if at all possible.

Appear quietly confident at all times

Businesses whose owners brag too much or too loudly tend to be looked upon with suspicion by their peers. There is always someone waiting in the wings to crow with glee when a braggart comes to a sticky end, so don't attract the wrong sort of attention. The British have always supported the little fellow, the underdog, or the person who struggles against great odds to become a winner, but they have also developed a knack of then wanting to see them brought down to size because they've become 'too big for their boots'. The word might be German, but the British could have invented the sentiment of *Schadenfreude*, which is the enjoyment of witnessing someone else's misfortune.

It usually benefits the business person to be perceived as someone who would rather keep out of the limelight, but who seems to have a quiet confidence in his or her abilities, business and direction. People like to deal with steady, solid businesses and their proprietors, because they can be confident that they will be there in future if anything goes wrong with the products or service. An added benefit is that less ostentatious cars and clothes are needed to keep up the image than might be necessary otherwise – more profits on the bottom line quietly to impress your audience, be they lenders, investors or customers.

If you find that you've had a particularly good month in your business, it might be prudent to keep that information to yourself initially, just in case you have to compensate for a real 'stinker' the following month!

Don't rely on anyone else 100%

It's extremely rare to find someone who can be relied upon 100%. You must always make allowances for people letting you down, in order to be able to react in time if, and when, it happens. It doesn't please us to have to say this, but we feel that it is an important contribution to staying in business. If someone promises you that they will supply you with the parts which you need desperately for an important piece of machinery, ask yourself 'What if they can't get these components here in time?' and make contingency plans.

There is no one in the world who is as committed as you are to the success of your business, who could benefit more if you get it right, or who stands to lose as much as you if you fail, so why should you expect others to try as hard as you?

Plan for disaster

You might think that you've put all the pieces of the jigsaw in place to guarantee you business success, but there are bound to be areas over which you have little or no control, generally in the supply of services, goods or materials which you will need to carry on your business. Ask yourself what areas present you with the greatest risk to your business if they go wrong, and try to work out a contingency plan to cope with the disasters which could strike. An example of this could be to make sure that you have at least two suppliers of materials, such as leather for bag manufacturing, which are critical to your production and supply of finished goods, and that you are never over-dependent on only one source.

Another potential disaster area is your overdraft facility, if you have one. Remember that this can be recalled at any time by the bank, if it feels that your business is showing all or some of the signs of failing, or if you fail to run your account satisfactorily, such as persistently writing cheques which you know cannot be met with the funds available at the time of issue. Having entered into a relationship with your bank, you have to meet their terms and conditions, otherwise you will find yourself spending much of your time fending off calls from your manager, writing reports and cash flow projections of your intention to reduce your borrowings. All of this is totally counter-productive and stressful, and removes your concentration from your core business activity at the most critical point.

Listen to your customers

Make a point of asking your customers for ways in which you could provide them with a better service, and then DO SOMETHING ABOUT IT! From a customer's viewpoint, the only thing worse than not being asked an opinion is having suggestions ignored. Having shown them how open you are and how you care about your service, please don't ruin the relationship by not acknowledging a positive comment. If the suggestions made are useful, implement them where possible. If the suggestion is impractical, let the customer know that you value their input, but explain why you are unable to use that particular suggestion at that time.

Don't just ask clients if they are satisfied or unsatisfied with your firm, ask what they think you could do to improve a particular service or product. Find out if they have difficulty getting other products or services which you do not currently provide for them, and establish whether or not adding them to the package offered would be mutually beneficial. If you can't provide help in this area yourself, try to provide them with a personal contact who can.

Get to know your customers, and how your products fit in to their overall picture. Make sure you understand how critical a part you play in the success of their business, and how you might be able to help them provide a better service to their customers.

Honesty is the best policy

If you find yourself in a difficult situation such as lack of funds due to late payers or bad debts, it is best to confront this sooner rather than later. If you have a good relationship with the bank, this will stand you in good stead. If you can illustrate that cash flow problems are temporary, you should be able to find a sympathetic ear. No matter how much planning you do, there will always be some problem waiting to catch you out. Since this happens to almost everyone in business at some time or other, it is nothing to be ashamed or embarrassed about. Make an appointment with the bank manager and meet him or her face to face – do not attempt to negotiate this kind of help over the phone. You may find that the experience of the bank manager helps you to identify another solution which is more appropriate, since money alone is not always what is needed.

If you have certain bills to pay which have become pressing, it is better to talk to the suppliers concerned and explain your problem frankly than to write a cheque which you know will bounce. Suppliers have probably suffered similar problems to yours from time to time, and are willing to arrange for debts to be paid in amounts that you can afford when the alternative is no payment at all, or lengthy and expensive legal proceedings. You might find that in order to keep your account open with a supplier, the outstanding debt is effectively frozen, to be repaid in instalments, and a fresh account is opened with less generous credit terms than previously, or even operated on a cash on delivery basis.

This is usually preferable for everyone, since it would probably serve no real purpose to stop trading with you altogether. Once the frozen debt has been cleared, you can probably start trading on the same credit terms as you had previously.

If, despite your disaster planning, you have problems with suppliers, for any reason, and these are affecting your ability to supply your own customers with your finished product or service, let your customers know what this implies for their stocks etc and allow them the opportunity to avoid problems which your situation might have otherwise caused for them. Since you should already be well aware of your importance in the eyes of your customers, any failure to react in time will reflect badly on you in future. The fact that you acted selflessly in order to protect your customer will stand you in good stead, since it is how you cope with a problem that is more important than the problem itself.

Don't run before you can walk

Many people who are new to business often fail to realize that it is just as easy for a business to run into difficulty because it has TOO MUCH work as it is because it has too little. If you blindly accept orders with little thought for scheduling and payment in line with your financial capacity, you are asking for trouble. If you have to fund the purchase of materials, standard rates of pay, overtime rates, etc. out of a limited budget, then there is precious little room for manoeuvre to cope with sudden increases in pressure in these areas due to unexpected business. That's why you have a business plan, of course, with an assessment of how much business you will need to be efficient, with allowances for some increase or decrease from the expected levels. Don't use up your working capital too quickly. Overtrading (as it is known) is a common cause of failure amongst over-eager entrepreneurs.

If you are offered unexpectedly high levels of business, it would be a wise move to discuss the matter with your bank before becoming contractually obligated. It may be that your local manager can put in place the extra facilities that you might require to take on this workload, but you will recall that in the early stages of a business's development, lending is usually backed by adequate personal security. If you have already pledged all the security that you have available, you might have to make an application to specialist sources, such as the Small Firms Loan Scheme. From experience, this is not terribly popular with the banks, but it is there specifically to provide loans where all available security has been taken up. Applications need the usual business plan and projections, so allow time for these to be prepared in addition to the time taken to consider and process your application.

If the business that you are in lends itself to invoice finance or factoring, this might be a quicker way of overcoming the collateral/security problem. As we discussed earlier, the value of the sales invoices and the credit worthiness of your clients provides the basis for the security of this form of finance. Factoring companies tend to favour certain industry sectors, minimum turnover levels, and types of contract. It is worth investigating in the early stages of your financial research, so that you will be aware in advance of the likely atttractiveness of your business to a factor, and at what level. This could also prove to be a faster way of putting your finances in place to take on unexpected medium-to-long-term contracts.

Stick to your plan

You will have invested a significant amount of time, and probably money, in the preparation of your business plan before coming up with the final article. The basic structure and scale of the plan will have been calculated by taking into consideration your available financial, technical and human resources. Try to stick to your plan unless there are overwhelming reasons for changing it. It is designed as your guide to the progress of your fledgling business, and is geared towards its success. Avoid the temptation to drift away from your chosen path because of boredom with the pace or content of your daily routine. If that's what you've allowed for, stick to it and keep things under control. If you find yourself being easily diverted, try to analyse the reasons why and make adjustments as you go along. Refer back to your Personal Statement of why you wanted to go into business in the first place, and ask whether or not taking a different direction will give you the ability to meet your original personal objectives.

Avoid the Time Robbers

The management of your time is absolutely critical to the success of your business. This is why you must not allow others to rob you of that most precious commodity. Time Robbers are those people who know how to while away a good half hour or more of someone else's time by drifting past, enquiring about the weekend's activity, the weather, the latest industry or office gossip, or any other subject but the work in hand! In addition to robbing you of your time, they also rob you of your attention, so that even once you get rid of them, it usually takes longer to get back into the right state of mind or train of thought.

It can be very difficult to avoid this completely, and no one wants to seem rude, but using verbal signals (short answers, grunts of agreement, etc.) or body language (picking up the phone to make a call) to show that you are too busy to spend too much time on idle chit-chat usually does the trick.

If it's a friend who's dropped by, you could arrange for staff or others to interrupt you with a phantom telephone call, or the need to make an urgent visit to the workshop. This should help them to take the hint! Make sure that your friends or family with time on their hands do not start to treat your workplace as a place to idle about in, drinking free tea and coffee all day. It's not only a potential waste of your time and money, it can demotivate your hard-working staff.

Ask yourself throughout the day 'Am I making the best possible use of my time right now?' If you're not – change what you're doing so that the answer can be 'Yes.'

Control the finances

Who will be authorized to sign cheques? The temptation is to keep this responsibility to yourself initially, but you will find that there are occasions when it would have been beneficial to have another signatory available such as when you need to be out of the office etc. A trustworthy secretary or personal assistant should be able to exercise his or her judgement in authorizing cheques for smallish sums (say up to £100) for stationery, sundry supplies etc, rather than delaying the purchase of something needed in a hurry. Obviously, you need to be confident that the funds are there to meet the cheques, and that your signatory will not be careless in needlessly paying out too early for such purchases.

Never lose sight of your bank balance, since this is the life-blood of your business. Start your day with a health-check of the financial position. This can be done by referring to your closing bank balance the night before or by accessing your account details directly. If you have the facility, this might be a simple phone call to your regular contact at your local branch to see what movement there is to be with previously banked or drawn cheques being cleared that day, and any standing orders or direct debits being paid or received. Banks are also moving toward providing clients with the facility to dial directly into their account in order to switch funds, make payments or simply review balances. A visit to your bank for a demonstration of any available system will tell you whether it could be of benefit to you. However, these systems are not necessarily cheap, so make sure you know of the full cost of having the service, and weigh up the financial pros and cons as well as the convenience factor before committing yourself to it. Try to obtain a free trial to put it through its paces first, if this is practical.

If your business operates mainly on a cash basis, your bank statement can form the basis of any management accounts which you might wish to keep. Beware of over-reliance on your bank statement, however, since it cannot show cheques in transit which you have written and sent but which have not yet cleared. It is simply a snapshot of your bank account at a given moment in time, and cannot provide sufficient information to monitor the true health of your business.

If you operate a petty cash system within your business, ensure that this too is kept under a reasonable degree of scrutiny, especially if large amounts are involved. Receipts should be produced where possible to back up your claim or that of employees, but use your discretion. Do not be tempted to use it like a personal bank unless you are prepared for the extra work involved in unravelling it at the end of a year. VAT, for example, is (normally) only reclaimable if the proper receipt has been produced.

You might have thought that a bank would automatically issue things like statements of annual interest paid or received, but experience tells us that this is not the case. You will probably have to apply in writing to request these every year. You are entitled to them, and the tax man will not allow you to claim interest as an expense to your business unless you can show proof in the form of a certificate from the bank. You should also request certificates of interest for your personal accounts, since from now on your personal finances will be inextricably linked with those of your business.

> Don't lose bank statements – they're expensive to replace!

The cost of banking

Without wishing to comment on the morality or justification for some of the charges made by banks, we feel that the budding entrepreneur should at least be aware of how the banks will be able to earn money from new (and existing) businesses. As well as interest on borrowed money, you should realise that banks want to charge you money for just about everything these days, but the main items to watch are:

- Annual Arrangement Fees to set up or renew overdrafts (around 1% of sum)
- One-off Arrangement Fees to set up term loans (around 1% of sum)
- Administration fees to cover work within their legal department when taking security over assets (several hundred pounds)
- Referral Fees for exceeding overdraft limits, where the bank honours a cheque it could have 'bounced' (around £15 to £25 per cheque)
- Excess interest charges at higher rates once overdraft limits have been exceeded (around 25% p.a.)
- Service Charges for operating the account: cheques, cash movements, electronic payments etc. (currently 10p to 50p per item, depending on the type of account, plus a percentage of the value of the cash, around 60p per £100)

There are even times when the bank will charge you for NOT borrowing money. When you become successful, and start playing around with sums in the millions, you might have occasion to negotiate an overdraft of say, £2 million for a specific purpose. You pay the arrangement fee, and the bank effectively sets aside the money for you. In the event that the deal you've been working on falls through, the bank may charge you money partly to compensate for any interest which it would have earned had you drawn down the cash. Bear this in mind – it might happen sooner than you think.

Sales, Purchase and Nominal Ledgers

These are the basic components of bookkeeping with which you will be confronted. It can be a fairly simple job to set up and control with the help of your accountant, but a potential nightmare if you attempt to do it on your own with no previous skill or experience in this area. We would suggest that at this stage it is sufficient for you to be aware that these things exist and will have to be kept. We highly recommend that you consult your accountant about setting up a simple system for you to keep, either manually or on a computerized system. By doing it this way you will be sure that the methods you will use will be compatible with his, and this should also keep your audit bill (if necessary) down at the end of the year. Contrary to popular belief, accountants do not enjoy charging small customers huge fees for unravelling a mess. They would prefer to keep you as a satisfied and solvent customer by working with you to keep your book-keeping clear and unfussy. You will probably find that the sooner you start to work along guidelines set by your accountant, the easier your relationship will be, and the less stress you will suffer in attempting to piece together parts of your business activity from memory when audit time comes around.

Do unto others ...

What is business all about? Is it about going for the kill, and taking advantage of other people's weaknesses? It may be like that for some, but for the majority of people in business

DO UNTO OTHERS ...

for themselves, and especially in the early stages, it's all about survival. If you want to get on with other people, treat them with respect, and don't do to them what you wouldn't want them to do to you.

Don't be shy about sprinkling your business life with small acts of kindness, such as opening doors to training or employment opportunities for the children of customers, or sending cards and flowers on birthdays and anniversaries. More importantly, don't look for anything in return. These things have a habit of repaying themselves in their own good time, and usually with far more than you could have wished.

APPENDIX

CHOOSING YOUR ADVISERS

Throughout this book we have suggested that you get appropriate advice at every stage of the planning and setting-up of your enterprise. Many people starting out in business on their own for the first time have little knowledge of business or financial administration, so it is essential that good advice is obtained from the very start.

Small businesses are big business today and the government, in particular, has set up a network of state funded organizations which can offer advice and assistance (see list at the end of this section). Most of the government organizations are staffed by professional people with considerable expertise, but they do not become personally involved in your business; their role is an advisory one.

There are, however, three professional advisers who may become much more closely involved with your business:

- accountant
- bank manager
- solicitor

Accountant

Even if you are not obliged to have an accountant, we strongly advise you to do so. At the outset a competent accountant can help you to

- identify appropriate sources of finance;
- compose a business plan;
- approach a lender.

Later, once your enterprise is up and running, your accountant wil give advice on:

- setting up books and records;
- registering for VAT, National Insurance, PAYE etc;
- setting up a system for preparing regular management reports.

In addition he/she will:

- prepare your accounts;
- deal with the Inland Revenue on your behalf;
- know how to obtain maximum tax benefits for your business.

How do I find an accountant?
You could ask your bank manager for his or her recommendation and, of course, friends and associates will be happy to give you the names of their accountant.
Visit potential firms, outline what kind of service you will need (be HONEST, or you could end paying more than you intended!) and ask for a guide to costs.

Robert Dallas, a practising accountant comments:
'I think it is essential for an accountant to advise the new business on arrangements with the bank, as banks are now so profit-driven and managers so geared to performing to targets that they will often offer a deal which could be knocked down with a bit of assistance.'

In the UK, at present, ANYONE can call him or herself an accountant or book-keeper, so be careful who you choose. Contact the Chartered Association of Certified Accountants and the Institute of Chartered Accountants (addresses at your local library) for lists of their members. Accountants who belong to these professional organizations have appropriate qualifications and experience and will adhere to the body's code of professional ethics.

Ask for a letter of engagement outlining what level of service has been agreed.

An accountant is not responsible for telling you how to run your business nor is he or she responsible to the Inland Revenue or other authorities for inaccuracies in the information supplied to the accountant by you or if you fail to disclose relevant information. Moreover YOU are responsible for checking the figures on all documents submitted to the tax, VAT, national insurance and other relevant authorities, not your accountant. Your accountant will help you to claim maximum tax relief and other benefits and can offer you advice, but ultimately YOU must take responsibility for the information given and the control of your company's finances.

Query what appear to be excessive bills and be prepared to take your business elsewhere if you are unhappy with explanations. Discuss problems with other business people.

Bank manager

Whether or not you decide to borrow from the bank you will almost certainly need to apply for a business account. If you are reasonably happy with your present banking arrangements then it makes sense to have your business account at the same branch, particularly if you have a good relationship with the manager and staff. (Though bear in mind our previous advice to keep your private and business finances separate, if possible). Banking at a local branch may seem unnecessary in these days of high-tech telecommunications, but you are more likely to be able to pop in frequently and the manager will have local expertise.

It is worth bearing in mind, however, that High Street banking is becoming fiercely competitive, and more and more banks are vying for the rapidly growing small business trade. In addition, some of the larger building societies now offer cheque accounts and may also offer higher rates of interest on deposit accounts than the banks. All the banks and building societies produce quantities of leaflets detailing the services they offer, so it makes sense to collect and read as many of these as you can, so that you can make an informed choice.

As well as becoming more competitive, the banks rely heavily today on what is known as 'criteria-based lending'. What this means in practice is that the friendly, knowledgeable and highly-experienced older manager, often with wide local expertise, has largely been replaced by a younger version, possibly with less experience and local knowledge. And whereas decisions to lend were once based not only on the facts and figures, but also on the client's personality, reputation and achievements, today they are more likely to depend much more heavily on security, ability to repay, cash flow projections and so on. The ultimate effect of this means that there is less flexibility for smaller customers.

Establishing a good relationship with your bank is extremely important; if you are open and honest in your dealings with the bank, the bank is more likely to listen sympathetically if things go wrong.

- Ensure that you are informed and prepared when you meet the manager to discuss your business.
- Be prepared to listen carefully to what the manager says, even if it's not what you want to hear!
- If you do obtain finance from the bank, ensure that you understand all the implications.
- Be aware that interest rates can vary and overdraft facilities can be stopped very quickly.
- Make sure you understand all the charges that will be made on your business account before you agree to go ahead.

- NEVER allow yourself to become aggressive or abusive with the bank manager; it will not solve anything and will only make matters worse.

Mutual respect is the keynote of any good relationship.

Solicitors

Solicitors can deal with a wide range of matters such as employment contracts, partnership agreements, the collection of bad debts, buying and selling property, obtaining licences and so on. You may already have a family lawyer with whom you are on good terms, but it is worth checking that the partners have adequate commercial experience. If not, they will probably be able to recommend a suitable firm to you. And you can ask friends and business associates for their advice.

Once you have chosen a solicitor you should meet and talk over your initial plans (take along your Business Plan). He or she can advise you of any legal aspects you should know about and you can discuss a scale of charges.

LIST OF USEFUL ORGANIZATIONS

Training and Enterprise Councils and Local Enterprise Companies

Established in 1991 as the result of a government initiative, the TECs (in England and Wales) and the LECs (in Scotland) now form a network of offices across the country. The services offered by each TEC and LEC vary according to local needs. All offer free information, advice and training. TECs and LECs also run various schemes such as the:

Business Start-Up Scheme which offers direct financial assistance, as a weekly allowance, together with training and counselling to unemployed people who wish to start their own business.

Business Advisory Services (BAS), an information and counselling service to help small and growing businesses.

Telephone the Department of Trade and Industry (DTI) Enterprise Initiative on 0800 500200 to find the name of your local TEC/LEC. See also below, *Local Enterprise Agencies and Enterprise Trusts*.

Local Enterprise Agencies and Enterprise Trusts

There are now some 400 LEAs (England and Wales) and Enterprise Trusts (Scotland) which fall under the auspices of the TECs and LECs and are sponsored by the government, local authority and a network of local businesses and banks. Their aim is to encourage business start-ups and help them to survive and be profitable. LEAs and Enterprise Trusts can give independent and confidential advice on such issues as marketing, exporting, accounting, tax, insurance and manufacturing, as well as general counselling. In addition, some provide workshop space or office premises and secretarial and administration services.

Business Links (England), The Scottish Business Shop, Business Centres (Wales). (For Northern Ireland see below)

With offices in major towns and cities, these government-sponsored organizations are a 'one-stop shop' for business services. They can offer free advice on a wide range of issues such as:

Business strategy and change

Financial management, late payment, taxation and availability of grants

Training and development

Business start-up

Business information and databases

Export services

Consultancy

Innovation, quality, design and technical services

Business skills services

Personal business advisers respond directly to their clients' needs; you can obtain advice by telephone or visit personally. Anyone without much previous experience of running a business is strongly advised to contact their local office and talk over their plans in a friendly, informal and helpful atmosphere. Your local Chamber of Commerce or TEC/LEC can give you the number of your Business Link/Business Shop. Or contact the DTI Enterprise Initiative (0800 500200).

Northern Ireland

Northern Ireland has its own *Local Enterprise Development Units* to promote, establish and develop small businesses. There are Regional Offices in Belfast, Londonderry, Ballymena, Newtownards, Newry and Omagh. Local Enterprise Agencies offer managed workspace and a range of business support services. Contact your regional Local Enterprise Development Unit to find the nearest LEA.

Companies House

Crown Way, Cardiff CF4 3U2.

Companies House offers a wide range of information on British business and a variety of useful publications which include the *31 Notes for Guidance*, easy to understand guides to the Companies Act and other regulations. Other brochures offer advice on *Choosing a Company Name, European Economic Interest Groupings, Company Secretaries' Duties and Responsibilities, Accounting Reference Dates* and *Liquidation and Insolvency*.

Companies House also holds the records of over one million companies and the on-line service, Companies House Direct, is a fast, inexpensive way of obtaining up-to-date company information via the Mercury network, directly to your personal computer. Scotland and Northern Ireland each have their own Companies House, in Edinburgh and Belfast.

Chambers of Commerce

Your regional Chamber of Commerce is a mine of useful information and its services include company searches, credit checks and news databases giving access to information on markets, products, services and countries. There are also opportunities, through seminars, meetings and travel, to make contact with other businessmen and women.

The Department of Trade and Industry (DTI)

The DTI (Ashdown House, 123 Victoria Street, London; General Enquiries 0171-215 5000) can give expert advice and help to firms of all sizes. The Business in Europe Office gives general marketing information and practical advice for companies wishing to trade in Europe. Overseas Trade Services (run in partnership with the Foreign and Commonwealth Office) is aimed at the smaller, less experienced exporter and can give marketing and trading conditions information for individual countries.

The DTI also offers help for smaller firms to obtain funding to take part in overseas trade fairs, seminars, product promotion and so on. Its Enterprise Initiative Linkline 0800 500200 can give you the telephone number of your nearest TEC/LEC (see above).

The Prince's Youth Business Trust

If you are aged between 18 and 29, the Prince's Youth Business Trust can give you business and marketing advice and, possibly, financial assistance to help you get started.

The Inland Revenue

The Inland Revenue runs a network of Tax Enquiry Offices (under Inland Revenue in the telephone book). You can contact an adviser by telephone or visit the centre. All advice is free and confidential. A wide range of booklets, leaflets and videos is available.

Department of Social Security (DSS) (National Insurance Queries)

Look under Social Security in the telephone book for the free Social Security Advice Line for Employers if you have a query about your employees' contributions. The local Contributions Agency Office advice centre can give information and advice about your own contributions. Remember to keep relevant National Insurance numbers handy when you call.

Advisory, Conciliation and Arbitration Service (ACAS)

ACAS has established a nationwide network of telephone enquiry points where you can obtain free information on employment issues, brochures etc. in strict confidence. ACAS also advises on manpower planning, recruitment, payment systems and incentive schemes.

SPECIMEN CONTRACT OF EMPLOYMENT

Note: This sample contract of employment is copyright and should be used for guidance only. Your solicitor can help you to formulate a standard contract for your particular business, and we strongly advise that legal help is obtained in preparing any kind of contract for your business.

FULL NAME
NATIONAL INSURANCE NUMBER

STATEMENT OF PARTICULARS FOR THE CONTRACT OF EMPLOYMENT
STATEMENT OF TERMS

(PURSUANT TO SECTION 1)
(THE EMPLOYMENT PROTECTION (CONSOLIDATION) ACT 1978)

This Statement dated..........................., sets out certain particulars of the conditions offered under the Contract of Employment that is currently in force in this Company.

1. Employment is offered under the terms and conditions of the Contract of Employment to:
(Name)..
2. Your employer is (Name)...............................
3. The job title is...

4. Your employment will be with effect from (date)................

5. Your basic remuneration will be paid monthly by cheque on the last working day of each month.

6. A probationary period of 6 months is agreed during which period this contract of employment may be terminated by either party summarily.

7. After satisfactory completion of the probationary period, the contract may only be terminated by either party giving written notice of not less than the period set out in the Employment Protection (Consolidation) Act – except by mutual agreement between the parties – payment in lieu by the employer for example.

8. The normal working hours shall consist of.........working hours.

9. The normal working hours shall be (times)..................

10. Holidays and Statutory Holidays will be in accordance with the appendices to the contract of employment held in the General Register of the employer, and to be read by the newly appointed as soon as is reasonably practicable.

11. Ill-health and absence through sickness and injury will be in accordance with the appendices to the contract, and the rules of the Company.

12. The full Contract of Employment is held in the General Register of the undertaking and will be read and noted by you on the commencement of your employment. This full Contract contains the appropriate appendices that relate to disciplinary rules and the grievance procedures as they are operated and observed by this undertaking. You will be permitted to re-refer to these rules and procedures as and when necessary so as to

ensure your full awareness of them.

13. The Company will expect you to undertake such training as may, from time to time, be beneficial to the working of the Company.

14. The Terms and Conditions of the Contract will be subject to such variation as may be necessary to conform to any Legal or Statutory requirement from time to time in force. It may be necessary to alter Terms and Conditions for economic trading reasons. In such instances, the proposed alterations will be discussed with you in order that a mutual agreement may be reached as to these alterations.

15. You will undertake to co-operatively observe and carry out such principles, tasks and activities that are conducive to the aims and objects that are necessary so as to ensure the economic and trading success of the Company.

16. The Health and Safety at Work Act 1974 places a Statutory requirement on the employer to ensure the health, safety and welfare of all who are employed by the Company, and to third parties who might be affected by any process or activity from within the undertaking and its operations. YOU will be expected to adopt the specific burden laid upon you by Section 7 of the Act – this section requires you to observe the safety rules and the appropriate regulations under the Act. This is explained in the appendices to the Full Contract of Employment, and should be specially noted by you.

17. You will be directly responsible whilst at work to:..................

Employees' Signature..Date..............
Employers' Signature..Date..............

The Contract of Employment

APPENDIX A STATEMENT OF GENERAL POLICY

1. The main aim and purpose of the undertaking is to provide, within the means at its disposal, such goods and services as are required, at prices and charges which are attractive, and at costs which will produce a sufficient margin to allow for satisfactory investment and development of the undertaking, and the payment of good and equitable financial rewards to the employees who earn them.

2. It shall be the duty of all employed, irrespective of function, seniority or status, to further the aims and objectives of the undertaking; to accept that we must succeed in our objectives for the ultimate benefit of all who are associated with the undertaking.

3. All persons so employed shall recognize that harmonious relationships are a vital ingredient, which combined with the efficient operation of well-maintained equipment, a constant vigilance over systems and methods, and the energetic application of personal expertise in all fields of activity, will ensure the continuity of employment within this undertaking.

4. The following conditions, codes and procedures are designed to establish and maintain good relationships, and to underwrite the intention of all concerned to sustain a spirit of teamwork throughout the enterprise. They are intended to be within the spirit and letter of all known employment legislation.

5. All persons who are joining the undertaking shall read this whole document and readily accept and observe its terms and principles in full. Failure to read and digest the contents of this

Contract will be no excuse in the event that the employee breaches any terms of the employment and faces disciplinary action.

6. Copies shall readily be made available for reference to any employee who requests to have further sight of appendices.

APPENDIX B CONDITIONS OF WORK

1. The Company shall provide the best conditions of work within its resources, conducive to the fulfilment of its objectives, and that are obligatory under the law and regulations as applicable to the industry.

2. Subject to the above, resources shall not be wastefully expended on facilities and convenience which have no recognizable benefit to the operational efficiency of the undertaking.

3. All persons joining the staff – in whatever capacity – shall within reason, be prepared to work on functions outside their designated employment as and when the need arises, so long as such work lies within their ability and skill.

4. Rates of pay and conditions will not be lower than those stated in the Contract of Employment – unless mutually agreed by the employer and employee so affected.

5. It shall be the duty of all employees to reach, maintain and practice high standards of personal ability, and to keep abreast of developments which may affect their sphere of work.

6. All employees shall themselves observe all SAFETY AT WORK Codes of Practice and, in particular, Section 7 of the Health and Safety at Work Act 1974, and to encourage others to

direct themselves likewise. The prosperity of the undertaking depends, to a large extent, on the safe and healthy condition of the workplace. The Company Health and Safety Policy and the Statement of Intent are available to all employees at all times.

THE WORKING OF OVERTIME There may be times when employees will be required to work overtime. Payment will be negotiated in line with the policy of the Company.

APPENDIX C GENERAL IN-COMPANY COMMUNICATION
1. INDIVIDUAL REPRESENTATION
1. Any regular employee wishing to make an enquiry, complaint or suggestion, or raise any matter relating to their employment, shall first state their case to the immediate supervisor, who will immediately advise whether or not the matter falls within the scope of that supervisor's authority. If it does, then the supervisor concerned shall make every endeavour to conclude the matter to the mutual satisfaction of both parties.

2. If the matter in question does not fall within the scope, or if mutual satisfaction is not reached, the supervisor shall arrange – without delay – for the employee to meet the next higher or senior authority within the undertaking. If requested by the employee, and only if so requested, the supervisor shall be present at the interview, and assist the employee to put the matter forward. If the employee wishes to be accompanied by a person other than the supervisor, any other regular employee can be chosen, if they are able and willing to attend.

2. COLLECTIVE REPRESENTATION

Any group of employees having a common or mutual enquiry, suggestion or complaint, or wishing to raise any matter relating to their employment – pay or conditions of work – shall first make their immediate supervisor aware of it, and request an interview with a senior authority of the Company. The person shall receive a small number of employees, who have been selected from those wishing to ventilate the matter, and shall advise as to whether the matter falls within the scope of that level of management. If the matter so falls, then a speedy endeavour will be made to mutually resolve the matter within the policy and objectives of the undertaking.

3. INDIVIDUAL OR COLLECTIVE

If mutual satisfaction cannot be achieved under 1 and 2 above, as the case may be, the whole matter shall be referred without delay to the highest authority within the undertaking, and urgent endeavour shall be made by all concerned to reach a mutually satisfactory solution.

4. Failure to reach a solution shall be mutually recorded, and the services of the ARBITRATION, CONCILIATION AND ADVISORY SERVICE (ACAS) shall be sought.

5. Normal working shall continue unhindered by actions or omissions of the employer or the employees during the currency of any part of this procedure for discussion, and all parties shall ensure that the client/customer/general services of the undertaking are guaranteed and complied with in total.

6. MEMBERSHIP OF TRADE UNIONS OR ASSOCIATIONS

Every member of the workforce shall have the right to join any trade union or association that would be appropriate to the industry. The Company reserves the right as to whether or not recognition of any trade union or association will be granted. Any 'closed shop' agreement that might have applied to this particular undertaking is null and void in line with the Statutory requirements so stipulated.

7. Membership of a trade union or an association shall not require a prior demand on the particular employee's loyalty and contractual duty to the undertaking.

APPENDIX D
HOLIDAYS AND SICK LEAVE
1. HOLIDAYS

Holiday with pay entitlement accrues on services rendered by the following formula:

From the date of commencement of official employment – that is to say, the ACTUAL day of starting, (2) days will be banked for the employee concerned, for each calendar month completed up to (24) days, which is the annual service entitlement. At a mutually agreed date, leave will be taken with pay in line with the policy of the undertaking and subject to the requirements of the department concerned.

2.STATUTORY HOLIDAYS

Following the date of commencement of employment, a day's

holiday with pay will be granted for each of the statutory holidays applicable to England/Wales/Scotland/Northern Ireland. If any of these days falls on a non-working day, an ad hoc arrangement will be operated – giving day or days in lieu, to mutually balance the entitlements to each employee concerned.

3. EMPLOYERS' SICK PAY SCHEME

Employees who are absent from employment because of sickness or injury due to an industrial accident, shall be subject to the provisions of the Statute and the rules thereto. It may be that the undertaking will make arrangements as to the amount of pay that can be made payable to an employee over and above the statutory rate. Lengthy or frequent periods of sickness shall be subject to Company monitoring and subject to any enquiry that the Company may wish to undertake, including possible 'second opinion' as to the ill-health leading to absence.

APPENDIX E CODE OF CONDUCT AND DISCIPLINE
THE COMPANY PROCEDURES

1. Every person who is employed within this organization shall read, learn and inwardly digest this appendix, as ignorance of the contents cannot be accepted as any mitigating circumstances in the event that any employee is in breach of them.

2. THE DISCIPLINARY CODE

i. Standards that are enjoyed by the employees, as measured by working conditions and financial rewards, resulting from conscientious and efficient work, shall not be jeopardised by the actions and failures of others.

ii. The objective of THE DISCIPLINARY CODE shall be the protection of the undertaking, and its business, and including all persons employed, from the adverse effects of inefficiency, negligence or unsatisfactory conduct of individuals, whether the cause of the adverse effects are as a result of either incapacity or particular harmful attitudes on the part of any employee.

iii. Those responsible for implementing THE DISCIPLINARY CODE shall normally have as their priority, the securing of the offender's cooperation in ensuring that there is no recurrence of an offence.

3. OFFENCES

Any attitude, act or omission which is contrary to the maintenance of good order, or could adversely affect the efficient working of the undertaking, or could place an unfair burden upon other employees is offensive behaviour, and will be dealt with in line with the following disciplinary Rules and Procedures. A list of the main areas that are viewed as offensive and as a breach of the employment contract is as follows:

a. Any failure to carry out accepted methods of operation – whether involving plant or machinery or systems of work.

b. Any failure to maintain responsible attitudes in personal acts.

c. Any failure to carry out known duties and responsibilities.

d. Unpunctuality, time clock fraud, leaving work early without authority.

e. Absence from employment without justifiable means.

f. Any act or omission being, or supporting, or leading to, or condoning an illegality, or contrary to policy of the undertaking.

g. Any failure to carry out a reasonable order or instruction that is reasonably given by an appropriate authority.

h. Misuse of any equipment or machinery, company property or anything under the control of the undertaking.

i. Acts of violence or personal abuse; dishonesty or theft.

j. For any employee to be under the influence of drink or drugs whilst at work.

k. Any failure to observe and encourage the principles of health and safety at work to the standards that are required at law.

4. PENALTIES FOR ANY BREACH OF THE RULES

Any penalties that are imposed shall be such as the imposing authority deems fair and reasonable, and that are appropriate to the particular breach of the rules, and will normally follow the stages listed below:

a. A VERBAL warning

b. A FIRST WRITTEN warning

c. A SECOND WRITTEN warning

d. A FINAL WRITTEN warning

e. Suspension with pay – pending an enquiry

f. Suspension without pay – pending an enquiry

g. DISMISSAL – or, with the consent of the employee concerned, and after due consideration, a disciplinary demotion; only in extenuating circumstances and, it must be emphasized, by agreement.

5. DISMISSAL: SUMMARY DISMISSAL OR WITH DUE NOTICE

The liability to dismissal may be incurred by an individual for any of the following breaches of contract. The list is not exhaustive, but is intended to illustrate to the employee the most obvious areas of risk.

a. Incompetence – especially after the probationary period.

b. Failure to reach, or maintain, the necessary standards as required.

c. False statements subsequently discovered in the 'job application'.

d. Gross negligence.

e. A deliberate or premeditated offence.

f. Dishonesty or theft, that is reasonably suspected by the employer after proper enquiry and procedural investigation.

g. Repeated offences, whatever the category of offence.

h. Any failure to comply with the terms of a Final Written Warning.

i. The commission of an offence of such gravity that continued employment of the offender would be incompatible with the maintainance of normal employee relationships.

j. Any breach of SECTION 7 of the Health and Safety at Work Act 1974, which reads as follows:

SECTION 7 THE HEALTH AND SAFETY AT WORK ACT 1974

'It shall be the duty of every employee while at work:

a) to take reasonable care for the health and safety of himself and of other persons who may be affected by his acts or omissions at work;

b) as regards any duty or requirement imposed on his employer or any other person by or under any of the relevant statutory provisions, to cooperate with him so far as is necessary to enable that duty or requirement to be performed or complied with.'

ALL EMPLOYEES SHOULD NOTE THIS SECTION. IGNORANCE OF ITS PROVISIONS WILL NOT BE AN ACCEPTABLE EXCUSE IN THE EVENT OF BREACH.

6. WRITTEN STATEMENT

Whenever a penalty is imposed, the imposing authority shall ensure that a WRITTEN statement, showing the offence and the penalty, is issued to the offending employee, and that a copy of the statement is placed in the employee's personal file.

7. PROBATIONARY EMPLOYMENT (as expressed in the Statement of Particulars)

During the employee's probationary period of employment, the immediate supervisor may impose – in the case of an offence – such restriction or penalty as appropriate in the circumstances. In the case of a serious or deliberate offence, or a repetition of offences, the details shall be reported to the senior authority, who will exercise judgement as to whether the employment of the probationary employee shall be terminated.

THERE SHALL BE NO RIGHT OF APPEAL AGAINST A PENALTY IMPOSED DURING ANY PART OF THE PROBATIONARY PERIOD.

8. GRIEVANCE HANDLING
Any regular employee who is aggrieved by the imposition of a penalty is entitled to invoke the procedure for employees, and have the grievance dealt with as is the procedure for complaints.

9. The whole of the procedure shall be carried out as expeditiously as circumstances allow, and in such a manner that will involve minimum interference with the normal functions of the undertaking.

10. At any time after two years service from the date of the penalty, the employee may request – through the procedure for employees – to have that recorded offence expunged from his or her personnel record, or, after any such period as the Company may decree.

11. REDUNDANCY
Subject to the economic and trading requirements of the undertaking, a policy of LAST IN–FIRST OUT shall be the guiding principle. In the circumstances of a surplus of employees becoming unavoidable internally, then the appropriate current legislation relating to redundancy will be observed. The Transfer of Undertakings as is expressed in EU legislation, and accepted by the United Kingdom as of 1981, is also recognized by this undertaking, and it will apply in the event that the undertaking becomes involved in such matters. HIGHLY SKILLED EMPLOYEES MAY REQUIRE TO BE SUBJECT TO SPECIAL REQUIREMENTS AND ARRANGEMENTS IF

REDUNDANCY SHOULD BE AN ISSUE. IN THE INTEREST OF ALL, THE RELATIVE EFFICIENCY AND SUITABILITY OF EMPLOYEES WILL BE TAKEN INTO ACCOUNT.

12. Redundancy counselling may be available should any employee require it. The trauma associated with certain cases of redundancy can be mitigated by such counselling, especially when long-service employees are in this position. The undertaking's policy on all matters that affect the employees is one of equity and consideration.

THE HEALTH AND SAFETY AT WORK ACT 1974

THE GENERAL DUTIES

THE EMPLOYER AND THE EMPLOYEES

1. GENERAL DUTIES OF EMPLOYERS TO THEIR EMPLOYEES

(i) It shall be the duty of every employer to ensure, so far as is reasonably practicable, the health, safety and welfare at work of all employees.

(ii) Without prejudice to the generality of an employer's duty under the preceding subsection, the matters to which that duty extends include in particular:

a. the provision and maintenance of plant and systems of work that are, so far as is reasonably practicable, safe and without risks to health;

b. arrangements for ensuring, so far as is reasonably practicable, safety and absence of risks to health in connection with the use, handling, storage and transport of articles and substances;

c. the provision of such information, instruction, training and supervision as is necessary to ensure, so far as is reasonably practicable, the health and safety at work of all employees;

d. so far as is reasonably practicable as regards any place of work under the employer's control, the maintenance of it in a condition that is safe and without risks to health and the provision and maintenance of means of access to and egress from it that are safe and without such risks;

e. the provision and maintenance of a working environment for employees that is, so far as is reasonably practicable, safe without risks to health, and adequate as regards facilities and arrangements for their welfare at work.

2.GENERAL DUTIES OF EMPLOYEES AT WORK

It shall be the duty of every employee while at work:

a. to take reasonable care for the health and safety of himself/herself and of other persons who may be affected by his or her acts or omissions at work;

b. as regards any duty or requirement imposed on the employer or any other person by or under any of the relevant statutory provisions, to cooperate with the employer so far as is necessary to enable that duty or requirement to be performed or complied with.

SPECIMEN BUSINESS PLAN
PLEASE NOTE THIS BUSINESS PLAN IS COPYRIGHT AND IS
INTENDED ONLY AS A GUIDE

Local Enterprise Agencies/Enterprise Trusts can usually supply
examples of Business Plans appropriate for various kinds of
business start-up projects.

<u>PLM SERVICES</u>

BUSINESS PLAN

CONTENTS

1. Description of Business

2. Development of the Business 1996/1997

3. Details of the Project

DESCRIPTION OF BUSINESS
1.1 Range of Services
The Company aims to provide a package of support services for
clients which will allow the management of those businesses to
become more efficient and productive in their primary function.

272

These services will cover:

Marketing
Public relations
Payroll
Book-keeping
VAT return preparation
Management Accounts preparation
Administration services
Health and Safety compliance
Employment legislation
Computer systems awareness and training

1.2 Management Team

A.B. (47) is a chartered accountant with over 25 years' experience in private practice who lectures in accountancy at degree and professional level in Anytown. He will assist in setting up accounting and management reporting systems, and recruitment of suitably qualified staff.

C.D. (36) has 15 years' experience in sales and marketing management within manufacture and distribution, and has lectured in Business Studies and Distribution in Further Education.

E.F. (45) is a civil engineer with over 20 years' experience in management and administration of small business.

Three full-time positions are to be created initially, with an additional four full-time posts to follow as the business develops.

1.3 Turnover in Relation to Services

In order to service the requirements of the clients, it is forecast that turnover will be generated in the following ratios:

A. Marketing and Public Relations   40%

B. Administration   30%

C. Book-keeping/accounts   30%

1.4 Markets Serviced

The Company is targeting small, family-owned businesses involved in manufacturing, and some building services clients who service the requirements of manufacturing and other clients of their own.

Generally, clients will be expert in the core activities of their business, but could benefit significantly from a wider range of experienced advisers working closely with their business, bringing higher levels of expertise in management techniques.

1.5 Market Share

In order to provide an efficient package of services, the Company requires a minimum of four clients. Ten clients would provide a sound customer base, and existing resources could cope with a maximum of twenty clients. These figures represent a very small proportion of the total number of small businesses which could make use of the services offered. Accurate percentages will be made available once details can be obtained from Anyshire Regional Council's business database.

1.6 Major Customers
Agreement has already been reached to provide services to the following clients:

A. PLS Ltd
B. Walsh & Son
C. Bingley, Baines
D. The Boston Organization

1.7 Major Competitors
In the main, competition comes from accountants and advertising agencies who provide only part of the range of services to be offered by the Company.
Clients are likely to be located in Anytown, Anyshire and Central England. It follows, therefore, that any accountant or advertising agency servicing small businesses will compete in part for clients' business.

1.8 Competitive Edge
As can be seen by the disparate nature of the competition, the Company offers clients a major benefit in providing a single contact point for a comprehensive range of services.
A major benefit to clients will be the development of a network of contacts, each bringing a wealth of business opportunities

which will be of interest to others. This network will allow clients to identify opportunities which might otherwise not be open to them, and to do so quickly.

The provision of expertise in the areas specified means that the client is able to concentrate on those aspects of his core business which generate the profit required for the successful development of his business.

Since most businesses need to show profits in order to meet the lending criteria of banks and other lenders, the package of services allows clients to be able to demonstrate their current level of business trading and profitability. By doing so, a business becomes a more immediate and attractive lending proposition when negotiating funds for expansion.

1.9 Marketing

Because of the small numbers of clients required, the company hopes to recruit the majority of its clients by referrals from existing clients and introductions by third parties who are aware of the services and their suitability.

In addition, an appropriate corporate brochure will be produced which can be used for presentations at trade shows and directed to potential clients.

Selective mail-shots will be used to target an appropriate audience, and seminars and presentations will illustrate the benefits of company services to invited audiences from appropriate industries.

Cost-effective advertising in newspapers and magazines which address the needs of the business community will also be used, such as:

Local daily paper
Local evening paper
National dailies

2. DEVELOPMENT OF THE BUSINESS 1996/1997

2.1 The Business

From a small but stable start, the Company is expected to grow steadily to cope with clients up to a maximum of twenty businesses making full use of the range of services offered.

Initial commitment to staff and facilities mean that profits in Year One are expected to be low. In Year Two, with an expanded client base and steady income, and making full use of existing overheads and facilities, a larger share of the additional revenues will be profit.

This steady progression into profitability will allow the Company to take advantage of possible expansion opportunities which may be appropriate at that time.

2.2 The Market

The problems facing small businesses targeted by the Company are unlikely to change dramatically over the next two to three years. This means that the need which we seek to fulfil will continue. Indeed, we expect there to be a growth of companies offering the type of service offered by the Company, once the benefits of a 'One-stop Shop' become obvious, and the profit potential identified.

The Company might well be presented with the opportunity to develop further by offering franchises or licences to entrepreneurs who want to get involved in offering such a depth and range of services, with the benefit of the idea having been previously refined.

2.3 Future Services

A flexible approach will be adopted, should the need for services other than those on offer become in demand. However, due to the reasons stated in the above paragraph, no major changes are currently foreseen. Training of clients in certain aspects of their support activity such as the use of computers to provide detailed management information, become popular as clients expand towards the stage where more control is necessary in-house.

2.4 Effects on Future Profitability

It is unlikely that all clients will remain for the long term, since they must adapt to the requirements of their business activity. This could mean the employment of their own staff in-house. Provision of training services for those staff could provide additional profitable income.

Depending on the level of additional turnover from that source, future levels including training could be 120% of that achieved at the end of Year Two.

2.5 Market Research

The provision of this service is being led by demand from potential clients, and future projections are based upon an intimate knowledge of the problems facing small businesses in their day-to-day operation.

To date, no statistical research has been undertaken by the

Company, since large amounts of empirical data are available to support the assumptions of the management team, based on many years' experience which includes direct involvement in a small business.

In addition, the high failure-rate amongst small businesses indicates a requirement for the provision of up-to-date management information. Banks and other lenders often refer to the lack of information available when lending decisions are negative, and the provision of such accurate information as required indicates a willingness on the part of potential borrowers to cooperate with the banks, helping to create a more favourable lending/borrowing environment.

2.6 Risk Factors

Since the main reason for the Company being set up is to service a known demand for the services on offer, the risks facing the Company are smaller than those normally associated with a small business in the early stage of development. Fixed costs are minimized, with services and staff being provided as required to fulfil the needs of the business as it develops.

However, in the first year of trading, it is unlikely that profits will be substantial. Since there is no established pattern of trade for businesses offering this range of services, there might be areas which have to be considered more fully as the Company develops, such as the costs of sales due to higher than expected advertising and marketing costs.

3. DETAILS OF THE PROJECT

3.1 A Platform for Future Developments

It is hoped that the innovative nature of the project will mean that the expertise of providing such a package of services will become valuable intellectual property once the value of the service becomes quantifiable.

If this is the case, then not only will there be a worthwhile business established on a local (regional) basis, but it will provide a platform for the idea to be developed and distributed on a national basis.

In this scenario, the income from the original business could become secondary, since fees from franchising and management of the overall operation are likely to outstrip those currently projected.

Bearing in mind that there are huge numbers of small businesses which could benefit from such a service, and there are approximately seventeen regions throughout the UK which could be bases for franchises, the total number of new, permanent jobs created could be in excess of one hundred.

3.2 Variable Factors

Initial revenues are unlikely to vary much from those projected, due to commitments made from captive clients. Expansion of staff numbers will take place in step with demand for services, thus minimizing risks from incurring too high a staff cost.

If sales are found to be 20% less than projected, the project is able to adjust its costs to ensure minimal impact on profitability.